CONVERSATION AND DISCOURSE

# Conversation and Discourse

STRUCTURE AND INTERPRETATION

Edited by Paul Werth

ST. MARTIN'S PRESS NEW YORK

**Library of Congress Cataloging in Publication Data**

Main entry under title:
Conversation and discourse.
    "Papers from the Bristol Conference on Social Psychology
and Language, July 1979, and Pragmatics microfiche reprints."
    Includes index.
    1. Discourse analysis – Congresses. 2. Conversation –
Congresses. I. Werth, Paul. II. International Conference on
Social Psychology and Language, 1st, University of Bristol, 1979.
III. Pragmatics microfiche.
P302.C624 1981      401'.41     80-28490

ISBN 0-312-16941-8

# CONTENTS

... to provide any industrious conversationalist with a new stock for every social occasion

Aldous Huxley

# CONVERSATION AND DISCOURSE

# INTRODUCTION

A tale from the Arabian Nights has a number of blind sages assembled before an elephant with the task of describing this unknown creature. The first sage takes hold of the trunk, and declares the animal to be like a snake. A second catches hold of a leg and insists that the elephant is shaped like a tree. A third, feeling the enormous flanks of the animal, says that it must be rather like a whale, while a fourth, encountering a tusk, says that the creature is undoubtedly in the form of a lance. Apart from demonstrating the pitfalls of an incomplete inductive approach to scientific investigation (though at the same time we may well wonder what sort of deductive theory would predict the shape of an elephant), this parable has some significance for the modern study of conversation. Just as medieval elephantology was badly in need of the integrated view, so we may argue would the modern study of conversation benefit from a pooling of resources. The present volume is intended as a contribution to this cause.

The ordinary speaker finds conversation to be by far the easiest variety of language, and it is perhaps for this reason that its manifold, shifting and problematic nature has been overlooked for so long. The substance of conversation is **linguistic**; however, if the linguist applies the methods and rules of orthodox **syntactic** theory to conversation, he finds that not only is it full of performance errors of the merely mechanical sort — false starts, hesitations, stuttering, spoonerisms and the like — but that furthermore it contains constructions — elisions, 'semi-sentences', intersentential connections — which a grammar derived from sentences cannot handle. Similarly, ordinary truth-conditional **logic** cannot capture, without extensive modification, the network of assumptions and inferences permeating even the simplest of conversations.

Conversations occur in **social situations**, between participants bearing **social relationships** with each other, and having certain conversational **goals**, which can be viewed in terms of **social functions**. There are several methodologies clustering around this area of inquiry. Since social functions are realised by actions, one approach is by way of the classification of actions, or **speech acts**, and associated with the names of J.L. Austin and John Searle, both philosophers. A related tradition, though emanating from sociology rather than philosophy, is that of the ethnomethodologists, based on the seminal work of H. Sacks, E. Schegloff and G. Jefferson (1974). These scholars view conversation as a social activity, governed by certain conventions of behaviour: speakers take **turns**, and are sensitive to the rules for **holding the floor**, but within these turns, the **moves** look very much like the speech acts of the Austinian school. A third approach, with affinities to both of the others, arises out of the linguistic theories of Michael Halliday, and is particularly associated with the names of J. McH. Sinclair and M. Coulthard. A discourse is regarded as a hierarchical structure of exchanges, each consisting of a number of moves. This hierarchy is partly, though not completely, isomorphous with that of Text:Sentence: Clause:Phrase.

Conversational goals may also be viewed in terms of **intended meaning**. A conversational contribution, that is to say, is from this viewpoint a **message** having a **co-operative function**, i.e. it is an integral part of a jointly-entered contract to make sense. Again, there are at least two possible approaches taking this as the starting-point. Firstly, there is the work of Grice: messages, for Grice, mean what they say; and if what they say does not make sense in their context, then the listener is entitled to infer that they are insinuating something which *does* make sense. This notion has been termed **conversational implicature**, and it provides a machinery for 'reading between the lines'. The second approach is that of text-linguistics, or discourse-grammar. Strictly speaking, the term 'discourse-grammar' is a misnomer, since a grammar must exhibit both weak and strong generative capacity (i.e. it must be capable of generating both the complete set of expressions in the language and also the correct structural descriptions of them). It is feasible that a grammar might be designed to generate all and only the possible texts of, say, English, but hardly that it could also associate correct structural descriptions with them, since it is unlikely that texts have that kind of tightly-defined structure. A discourse-grammar, then, is an enhanced sentence-grammar, rather than a distinct device in its own right. In principle, text-linguistics is capable of bringing together many of the diverse approaches discussed here, since a fully-fledged theory of text must occur in conjunction with a theory of context.

The papers in this volume represent a cross-section of a diversity which reflects not lack of direction but the richness and many-faceted nature of the subject. I have attempted to impose some sort of intellectual division on the papers by sectioning them into description and experiment on the one hand, and theory and analysis on the other.

This sectioning cuts across the methodological variety which I have spoken of, and is a crude attempt to isolate two research attitudes, or strategies, observable in the projects represented in this volume: we might call these strategies empiricist *v.* rationalist, or inductive *v.* deductive; the distinction is not absolute, but is better thought of as an emphasis or orientation upon data and analysis respectively. However, in all of the papers we may discern the presence of both data, whether evidential or illustrative, and analysis, whether theory-governed or utilitarian.

Within this imposed dichotomy, however, most of the interested disciplines are represented in this volume: sociology, social psychology, cognitive psychology, linguistics, anthropology, and philosophical logic.

Michael Brenner's paper, 'Aspects of Conversational Structure in the Research Interview', is concerned with the interaction between interviewer and respondent in terms of Austinian speech-acts and the ethnomethodological concepts of negotiation and repair. Brenner examines research interviews as sequences of elicitation, response and feedback and, interestingly, also looks at cases where the interaction has broken down and requires repair. His approach is firmly founded upon the principle that conversations occur in social situations, but by coding each exchange in terms of the speech acts involved, he is able to achieve some degree of quantification and thus objectivity.

Allen Grimshaw's paper, '**Instrumentality** Selection in Naturally-Occurring Conversation', is concerned with **manipulative** communication, in which a **source** uses an **instrumentality** on a **goal** to achieve a desired **result**. Grimshaw is thus investigating that class of speech-acts which Austin called 'exercitives', 'the exercising of powers, rights, or influence' (1975: 150), though this is part of a larger project in which different theories and methodologies are focused upon the same complex speech event by anthropologists, linguists, psychologists and sociologists (the Multiple Analysis Project, or MAP). Even so, Grimshaw has space to present only a programme for research and a sample analysis of part of the MAP data. Like Brenner, his interest in the data is directed particularly towards the construction of social structure as manifested in the text and co-text, for example in terms of *unsuccessful* manipulations (i.e. breakdowns, requiring negotiation and repair).

The paper by Gordon Wells, Margaret MacLure and Martin Montgomery, 'Some Strategies for Sustaining Conversation', is one of two papers concerned with data from child language, but the only one to make use of the Sinclair-Coulthard categories of **discourse**, **exchange** and **move**. Since the authors are particularly interested in the orderly patterns of discourse acquired by the child, they set out to investigate the type of ordered sequence which Schegloff and Sacks called the 'adjacency pair' and, especially, complex examples in which adjacency pairs may be chained to or embedded within others. One such is the **continue** which is a response (i.e. the second half of an adjacency pair) which simultaneously initiates a fresh exchange: it therefore constitutes an exchange-linking device. Wells and his co-authors then relate this to the notion of **prospectiveness**, which in their work is a scalar property of moves, rating them in terms of their expectation of a response. Speakers have a range of prospectiveness available to them (and acquired as children), allowing them to sustain or stop conversations with varying degrees of effectiveness.

The other paper dealing with child language is Hazel Emslie and Rosemary Stevenson's paper on young children's use of referring expressions, and specifically, of the definite and indefinite articles. Their methodological orientation is, however, very different from that of Wells *et al.* Their data is experimental rather than observational, and their analysis is text-semantic (or perhaps -pragmatic) rather than taxonomic. They point out that the appropriate use of 'a' and 'the' presupposes that the speaker makes assumptions about his interlocutor's knowledge and constantly monitors the state of this knowledge, particularly that which the speaker shares. Using the picture-narration method, whereby one subject describes a narrative series of pictures to another who cannot see them, Emslie and Stevenson investigate story-series using **repeated** referents, **new** referents, and **incongruous** referents, respectively. This technique enables them to control the unfolding of reference in the narratives, and therefore to test the child's ability to assess his listener's knowledge of the context.

Section II opens with Marion Owen's paper 'Conversational Units and the Use of "Well . . ." '. Though many of the other contributions also show the profound influence of Sacks, Schegloff and Jefferson, Owen's is probably the most thoroughgoing application and development of their approach and methods in the volume. She begins by discussing the taxonomy of conversational units, starting with the more familiar **turn** and **move**, and then passing on to the larger units, **interchange** (more or less equivalent to the Sinclair-Coulthard 'exchange') and finally, the **section**. The smallest kind of interchange is the adjacency pair, also referred to in the papers by Brenner, Grimshaw, and Wells *et al.* Adjacency pairs are often, in the terminology of generative grammar, 'self-embedded', producing what Gail Jefferson has called a 'side-sequence'; this often constitutes a **remedial interchange**, since the function of the side-sequence may be to clarify the opening move (e.g. Question) before closing it (viz. by a Response). Sections, finally, are the grosser functional divisions into which conversations (as well as other forms of discourse) fall – for example, closing sequences. Owen then goes on to illustrate this system not merely by subjecting a recorded corpus to analysis in its terms (which could be an unrevealing exercise) but by using it to *explain* a linguistic phenomenon: namely, the occurrence of prefatory 'well . . .'. She ends her paper with a plea for the genuine study of context-dependent language (and paralanguage) and not merely of isolated sentences.

Chet Creider's 'Thematisation in Luo' is probably the most straight-forwardly linguistic paper in the collection, in the sense that, more than the Werth or Wilson-Sperber papers, it is founded upon the 'Standard Theory' of generative grammar. It is, furthermore, the only paper to deal with non-English – indeed, non-Indo-European – data. Creider is concerned with the (originally Prague School) notions of **theme** and **rheme**: the theme is the initial constituent of a sentence (often the subject, though by no means necessarily – and the times when the theme is not also the grammatical subject are, by and large, of most interest linguistically); the rheme constitutes the rest of the sentence. Creider describes a transformational rule (Thematisation) which has the effect of shifting any Noun Phrase to the front of its sentence. There are also other rules in Luo which move other constituents to the front of sentences, which suggests that this position – the theme – has some important function. Creider then relates these linguistic facts to the system of turn-taking: the theme marks the speaker's claim to have the floor, and announces the topic of his contribution.

The paper by Paul Werth on the concept of 'relevance' is partially concerned with equivalent English data to Creider's for Luo, in that the theme, unless discourse-initial, will relate to the preceding discourse. This is effected, according to Werth, by the machinery of **emphasis**, which is either **Focus** (new material), **Reduction** (repeated or predictable material) or **Contrast** (denial of previous material). These emphasis-types are linked together by a set of rules which operate in circumstances defined semantically and/or pragmatically over the text. Emphasis is viewed in Werth's paper as the essential machinery of **coherence** in a text, marking successive pieces of information as linked in various possible ways (one of which is the use of determiners – cf. Emslie and Stevenson). He then claims that relevance and coherence are the same thing, but relates this to the functional structure of conversation: 'the participants in a conversation keep track of coherence, and this is manifested in their use of the machinery of emphasis-placement . . .'. Conversational contributions consist of (sets of) propositions which are **negotiated** before acceptance. While they are being negotiated they are held in a temporary store, or 'pending file'; subsequently, they are accepted, by the process of **incrementation**, into the **information pool**, or **common ground**.

The paper by Deirdre Wilson and Dan Sperber is a re-examination of H. Paul Grice's Co-operative Principle and its maxims, the cornerstone of most recent work in pragmatics. They set out to investigate three questions: (i) the relationship between saying and implicating; (ii) the interpretation of figures of speech, such as irony and metaphor; (iii) the interrelationships of the maxims. With regard to (i), Wilson and Sperber show that the maxims are not used only to assess implicatures, but as is shown by the disambiguation of sentences by context, the maxims are also used in the interpretation of what is *said*. The problem with (ii), metaphor and irony, is that the 'real' meaning often cancels what is 'actually' said, and therefore Grice's approach cannot account for it: what is needed, say Wilson and Sperber, is a separate theory of rhetoric. Problem (iii) is handled by re-casting Grice's maxims into a single one: 'Be relevant'. Relevance is then defined in their terms as 'a relation between the proposition expressed by an utterance . . . and the set of propositions in the hearer's accessible memory'. (The similarity between this and Werth's definition is quite striking.)

Conversations, then, are co-operative social ventures. Because they are co-operative, participants try to make their contributions appropriate to what has gone before, and to encourage each other. Because they are social, participants try to negotiate both for their turns and for the subject-matter. And because they are ventures, participants have occasionally to clarify, to repair and to reformulate their contributions. All of these possibilities are touched on in the present volume. The papers by Brenner, Grimshaw, Emslie and Stevenson, and Werth were all presented at the Bristol conference on Social Psychology and Language in July, 1979. The conference was organized by W. Peter Robinson, Howard Giles and Philip Smith, to whom my thanks are due for their permission — and indeed encouragement — to gather together the papers on conversation and discourse into a single volume (including one plenary paper, that by Grimshaw). Two more papers — those by Creider, and Wilson and Sperber — first appeared in *Pragmatics Microfiche*; I should like to thank the editor, Steve Levinson, for his permission to print them again here. The remaining papers, specially commissioned for the present volume, are by Marion Owen (a revised version of a *Pragmatics Microfiche* paper), and by Wells, MacLure and Montgomery (a revised version of a paper due to appear in the Sixth LACUS forum proceedings). Finally my sincere thanks to Val Hunter, for typing beyond the call of duty and in the face of great odds.

Paul Werth,
Hull


## References

Austin, J.L. (1975) *How to Do Things with Words*, 2nd edn, Clarendon Press, Oxford

Part One
# DESCRIPTION AND EXPERIMENT

# 1 ASPECTS OF CONVERSATIONAL STRUCTURE IN THE RESEARCH INTERVIEW

Michael Brenner

## 1. Introduction

We owe to Austin (1975) the first systematic exposition of the thought that language use in social interaction does not just involve the exchange of messages, but constitutes in itself the performance of social actions. 'There is something which is *at the moment of uttering being done by the person uttering*' (Austin 1975: 60). As is well known, Austin thus differentiated the act *of* saying something, the locutionary act, from the act performed *in* saying something, the illocutionary act.

The illocutionary aspects of conversational interaction are of particular interest to social psychologists, as an analysis of conversations in terms of the actions performed by speech provides a detailed understanding of the various means and practices which participants employ in living and constructing social situations when they are predominantly conversational in kind. In this paper, I will submit one conversational situation, the research interview, to a form of Austinian analysis with just this aim, that is, of providing some insight into the action organisation of interview conversation. To this end, I will first look at some general characteristics of research interviewing; this will be followed by an empirical inspection of a set of household interviews.

## 2. Some General Characteristics of Research Interviewing

The research interview, which is used predominantly for the purposes of data collection in survey research, may be defined as a two-or-more-person conversation 'initiated by the interviewer for the specific purpose of obtaining research-relevant information and focused by him on content specified by research objectives of systematic description, prediction, or explanation'(Cannell and Kahn 1968: 527). This definition implies that the use of the research interview is constrained by a particular ideal of information gathering which is **measurement**. Adequacy of measurement in the research interview is entirely related to the quality of three factors: the questionnaire, the respondent and the interviewer.

Research interviewing usually involves the use of a structured questionnaire. This means that all questions and instruments, such as prompt cards, to be used in data collection are designed prior to interviewing and are grouped together to form a particular sequence. While all the measures to be employed in the interview situation are listed in, or are associated with, the questionnaire, it is only by means of interviewer-respondent interaction that the actual measurement can take place. This imposes particular constraints on respondent and interviewer. As regards the respondent, he must be competent and willing to act in the interview as desired by the researcher. As regards the interviewer, he must only use those interviewing techniques which do not affect the respondent other than in terms of facilitating his provision of adequate answers so that validity of measurement is maximised. In addition, in order to secure reliability of data collection, all interviewing performances must be equivalent in their social interactional organisation, thus necessitating the standardisation of interviewing techniques.

When the questionnaire is well designed and respondents and interviewers cooperate effectively, the measures obtained in a data collection programme may be regarded as adequate and equivalent which is, incidentally, a prerequisite for the statistical manipulations employed in data analysis. In the practice of research interviewing, it has often proved difficult, however, to achieve adequate measurement fully because of various forms of bias arising in the interview situation (see, for example, Sudman and Bradburn 1974). All sources of bias are invariably related to the questionnaire, the respondent and the interviewer as well as to the interactions between them. Common deficiencies of questionnaire design are, for example, related to the choice of vocabulary in the wording of questions, so that respondents cannot, or cannot fully or unambiguously, understand what is meant by the question, or to the provision of inadequate routing instructions, this resulting in respondents being asked questions which do not apply to them. Common sources of respondent bias relate, for example, to the inaccessibility to respondents of the information sought, because they cannot recall it or repress it for reasons of social desirability of question content, or to the lack of ability or willingness to report information as desired by the interviewer. Hyman *et al.* (1954) first elaborated the two common sources of interviewer bias. They pointed to the tacit operation of interviewer expectancies on answers, 'how the interviewer enters the situation with certain attitudes and beliefs, which operate to affect his perception of the respondent, his judgement of the response, and other relevant aspects of his behavior' (Hyman *et al.*

1954:138), and they stressed the importance of inadequate interviewer performance as a source of bias in terms of cheating and of asking, probing and recording errors (see Hyman *et al.* 1954: 225-74).

Among these sources of bias, interviewer bias can be avoided most effectively, as the interviewer's performance can be controlled well in advance by means of adequate instruction and training. This was demonstrated, for example, by Marquis and Cannell (1969) who conducted a reliability study of interviewer-respondent interaction based on 181 taped interviews conducted by four particularly well-trained interviewers on employment matters. The findings revealed a very low level of interviewer error. Other studies (Marquis 1967; Marquis and Cannell 1971) indicate that an adequate control over the interviewer's performance is not only likely to secure a high level of reliability, but also influences positively the level of valid information reporting.

Research into the biasing effects of inadequate interviewer performance, together with the wealth of practical experience in research interviewing accumulated since the emergence of survey research in the 1930s, have led to the development of particular 'Do's and Don'ts of interviewing' (Smith 1972: 59-61), or **rules** of interviewing, which, when followed, enable the interviewer to gather information, in the majority of instances, with maximum reliability and validity. I consider here only the main rules to be followed by the interviewer (I) in the actual process of administering the questionnaire to the respondent (R) (for further discussion see Brenner 1978). These rules are listed below, together with the reasons for their existence.

| Rule | Reason for Rule |
| --- | --- |
| I must read the questions as they are worded in the questionnaire. | To avoid alteration of question content and/or question form. |
| I must ask every question that applies to R. | To avoid missing data. |
| I must use prompt cards and other instruments where required. | To obtain the kinds of answers desired by the researcher. |
| I must only probe nondirectively. | To avoid implying or suggesting a particular answer or range of answers. |
| I must make sure that R has correctly understood an answer and that it is adequate. | To avoid misrepresentation arising from selective comprehension of R's answer and the acceptance of an inadequate answer. |
| I must not answer for R. | To avoid bias arising from I's judgement of the adequate answer. |

| Rule | Reason for Rule *(cont.)* |
|---|---|
| I must not seek or give unrelated information. | To avoid distracting R from answering the questions. |
| When R asks for clarification I must clarify nondirectively and in accordance with the question objectives. | As R indicates problems in understanding what is meant by a question or probe or instruction I must clarify; this must be done nondirectively and in accordance with the question objectives to avoid alteration of question content and/or form. |
| When R gives an inadequate answer I must act nondirectively (probe, repeat question, repeat instruction, clarify) towards obtaining an adequate answer. | To avoid inadequate answers being accepted. |

## 3. A Conversation Analysis of Interviewer-Respondent Interaction

Given that research interviewing should involve the following of rules, it is possible for any particular data collection programme to assess interviewer-respondent interaction in terms of rule-following and rule-breaching. Some time ago, for the purposes of such an assessment, I was able to participate in a survey conducted by an experienced social scientist at the University of Wales. The survey was concerned with problems of social mobility in an economically and infrastructurally deprived valley area of South Wales. The data collection involved an experienced field supervisor who was in charge of six female interviewers, ranging in age between 30 and 50 years approximately. An interview with part of the interviewing team after the data collection programme had been completed revealed that the interviewers had undergone various interviewer training courses during their careers; they had also been trained by their supervisor who was convinced that she had a 'decent team'. Given that the researcher was able to employ experienced interviewing staff, no particular training was provided. Prior to data collection, the interviewers were carefully instructed in the use of the questionnaire and in all other procedures related to the interviewing. In all, 197 interviews were carried out of which I obtained tape-recordings of over 60; of these, 60 were of sufficient quality to be considered in my subsequent analysis.

During the first run of the tapes, a number of interviews by each interviewer were transcribed. These interviews were then used to develop a set of codes to be employed in a systematic action-by-action assessment of the conversational transactions between interviewers, respondents and bystanders. The contribution of bystanders, by the way, is omitted from discussion in this paper. Once the repertoire of codes was established, covering the interviewers' rule-following and rule-breaching actions as well as any other actions occurring in question-answer sequences (or Q-A sequences, for short), all 60 interviews were coded for the first time. After the first coding run, the tapes were coded again to improve the validity and reliability of coding attributions. I should mention that the coding was carried out directly from the tapes, involving just myself as coder. However, when complex instances of interviewer-respondent interaction were encountered, these were first transcribed and then coded. Finally, a test on the validity and reliability of the coding was performed, coding for the third time two randomly selected interviews for each interviewer. This test revealed a 98.86 per cent validity and a 97.85 per cent completeness of the coding attributions made. This means that this study involves a small number of wrongly attributed and omitted actions. I will now list and describe the codes employed in the tape-recording analysis, restricting myself for the purposes of discussion in this paper.

| Code | Code Meaning | Example |
|---|---|---|
| Question asked as required. | I reads question as worded in the questionnaire and uses the appropriate card when necessary. | |
| Question asked with slight change. | I reads question essentially as worded in the questionnaire and uses the appropriate card when necessary. | Instead of asking 'Would you say that the Upper Afan had more community spirit than towns on the coast about the same or less?' I asks 'Would you say the Upper Afan had more community spirit than towns on the coast about the same or less?' |
| Question significantly altered. | I adds to, omits from or changes the wording of the question in such a way that the meaning and/or the design of the question is significantly altered. | Instead of asking 'How satisfied are you with the provision of shopping facilities in the Upper Afan?' I asks 'Are you satisfied with the shopping facilities?' |
| Question completely altered. | Instead of asking the question as worded in the questionnaire, I invents a different question. | Instead of asking 'How satisfied are you with the number of friends you are able to see?' I asks 'Are you satisfied that you don't have any friends you're able to see?' |

| Code | Code Meaning | Example *(cont.)* |
|------|--------------|-------------------|
| Question asked as directive probe. | I asks the question in such a way that a definite answer is suggested to R. | Instead of asking 'With whom have you been discussing moving?' I asks 'With whom did you discuss moving, your husband, isn't it?' |
| Question omitted by mistake. | I fails to ask a question as required. | |
| Appropriate card not used. | I fails to use the card required with the question. | |
| Adequate probing. | I probes nondirectively, that is, without implying a particular answer or range of answers. | I uses probes such as 'Anything else?', 'Any other reason?', 'Can you tell me more about it?' or 'In what way?' |
| I repeats the question. | Instead of probing or for some other reason I repeats the question. | |
| Inadequate probing. | I probes in a leading manner, that is, implies a particular range of answers which is smaller than the range of answers implied by the question. | In the context of the question 'How satisfied are you with the size of your house?' I probes 'Would you say that you are dissatisfied?'; in the context of the question 'How long does it take you to get to work and back each day?' I probes 'Does it take you longer than ten minutes or not?' |
| Directive probing based on R's information. | I suggests a definite answer inferred from information previously supplied by R. | I  How satisfied are you with the size of your house?<br>R  It's alright.<br>I  So you're quite satisfied I suppose, aren't you? |
| Directive probing based on I's inference. | I suggests a definite answer based on her own inference. | I  Where do you mainly do your shopping for food? (pause) In the village I expect, isn't it? |
| Probing unrelated to task. | I probes for information which is not required by the question. | I  Now what is your job?<br>R  Miner.<br>I  And do you like the job? |
| R answers adequately. | R gives an answer within the frame of answering required by the question. | I  How much rent do you pay for this flat?<br>R  Six pound a week. |

| Code | Code Meaning | Example |
|------|--------------|---------|
| R's information is inadequate. | R provides information which relates to the question but is outside the frame of answering required by the question. | I How often have you discussed moving from the Upper Afan recently?<br>R Well, we have discussed it. |
| R's information is irrelevant to the task. | R provides information which is independent of the question. | Instead of asking 'Do you own or have access to any of the following, a car a motor bike a bicycle a scooter or a van?' I performs thus:<br>I Do you own or have access to any of the following, well, you've got a car, haven't you?<br>R Yes.<br>I You're not interested in a bicycle, a motor bike, a scooter, or a van?<br>R No.<br>(The 'No' constitutes irrelevant information following probing unrelated to task) |
| R gives feedback. | R indicates acceptance, attention or understanding. | R Mm. |
| R requests clarification. | R indicates problems in understanding what is meant by a question or probe or instruction. | I How satisfied are you with the physical surroundings of the Upper Afan?<br>R What do you mean? |
| I repeats R's information. | I repeats information just provided by R. | R Satisfied.<br>I You're satisfied?<br>R Yes. |
| I gives feedback. | I indicates acceptance, attention or understanding. | I Yes. |
| I answers for R. | | I How satisfied are you with the shopping facilities in the Upper Afan?<br>R There is nothing here.<br>I So you're dissatisfied? |
| I clarifies adequately. | I states or explains the question objectives. | I How satisfied are you with the physical surroundings of the Upper Afan? |

| Code | Code Meaning | Example *(cont.)* |
|---|---|---|
| | | R  What do you mean? |
| | | I   Well um (pause) like the scenery (pause) landscape and so on. |
| I clarifies inadequately. | I fails to state or explain the question objectives. | A question implying 'In your discussions about moving . . .' is handled by I thus: |
| | | I   Now what sort of things have you been discussing (pause) most frequently? |
| | | R  Like what then? (pause) |
| | | I   Well, you see when we said with whom have you been discussing moving from the Upper Afan you said your husband and the councillor. Then the next question is what sorts of things have you been discussing most recently (pause). |
| | | R  Um (pause). |
| | | I   That's a general question. |
| | | R  Um jazz band decorating, I think (giggles). |
| I gives unrelated information. | I provides information which is irrelevant to the question. | In the context of the question 'How satisfied are you with the number of relatives you are able to see?': |
| | | R  I like people coming here. |
| | | I   Yes yes you like company yeah (pause) and that's how it should be isn't it? I think (pause) that's what's the matter with us all we (pause) the human beings are too far apart now I think, don't you? We've drifted away from one another. |
| I indicates closure of sequence. | I concludes the Q-A sequence by means of 'Right'. | R  I'm satisfied. |
| | | I   You're satisfied. |
| | | R  Mm. |
| | | I   Right. |

Before turning to a discussion of some of the findings, I will first illustrate, to a limited extent, the kind of action-by-action coding performed. Like many other conversational encounters, research interviewing sometimes involves the occurrence of simultaneous and overlapping speech. This poses, unlike pauses between utterances or contiguous utterances, some coding problems as the codes can be attributed to the flow of speech only in such a way that a single action is noted at a time. In the case of simultaneous speech, I decided therefore to code the most prominent speech layer, as in the following example where the interviewer, the less prominent speaker, gives feedback while the respondent answers:

I   And to where would you be most likely to move where would you be most likely to move if you did move? (pause)
R   Well the only place that I'd move is that I want the coast,
I                                ⁽Yes
R   the country somewhere, the south coast somewhere.
I                  ⁽Yes

Whilst the occurrence of simultaneous speech meant that one layer of talk had to be ignored, overlapping utterances had to be coded as if they were discrete, the former leading to the underreporting of actions and the latter to a distortion of the actual delivery structure of speech. As pausing phenomena and the contiguity of utterances were also ignored, this further contributed to some distortion in the coding of the real-time organisation of speech. I should also mention that incomplete utterances as well as requests for repetition of utterances were not coded, that is, they were treated as not occurring. Inaudible speech was, however, noted, as were those utterances which proved impossible to code either because of ambiguity or because none of the codes applied. Below, I give a typical example of interview conversation where simultaneous and overlapping speech, contiguity and untimed pauses are considered; brief action descriptions are also provided, this illustrating the coding approach.

| Action | Action Description |
|---|---|
| I   And how satisfied are you with the physical surroundings of the Upper Afan? (pause) It's that card here (pause) satisfied (pause) very satisfied (pause) can you take these answers because otherwise you know | I asks question as required. |
| R                                ⁽Yes | Not coded. |
| R   Say that question again | Not coded. |
| I   Yes (pause) how satisfied are you | Not coded. |

| Action | Action Description *(cont.)* |
|---|---|
| | with the physical surroundings of the Upper Afan? (pause) | |
| R | What do you mean? | R requests clarification. |
| I | Well um (pause) like the scenery (pause) landscape and so on | I clarifies adequately. |
| R | (Good scenery isn't it now | R's information is inadequate. |
| I | (inaudible) | Coded appropriately. |
| R | Fine by the sea area isn't it? | R's information is inadequate. |
| I | (No we want the physical surroundings= | I clarifies adequately. |
| R | =Yes that's not too difficult you couldn't find it better anywhere else | R's information is inadequate. |
| I | So (pause) what would your answer be? | I probes adequately. |
| R | Satisfied | R answers adequately. |
| I | Satisfied | I repeats R's information. |

There were some Q-A sequences which were omitted as the majority of utterances proved uncodable. This turned out to be the ultimate limit of my coding approach, as indicated in the example below.

| Action | Action Description |
|---|---|
| I | How much does it cost to get back (pause) to work and back each day (pause) so of course it's petrol really now isn't it? (pause) How | I asks question with slight change and ? |
| R | (Yeah | Not coded. |
| I | many miles that you carry then? (pause) Five? Five (pause) and five back= | I ? |
| R | =Mm | R gives feedback. |
| I | So that's in all ten miles | I ? |
| R | (Ten in a day | R ? |
| I | Um= | Not coded. |
| R | =So fifty in five days is it? Right | R ? |
| I | Yes fifty miles (pause) so it's between one and two gallons a= | I ? |
| R | =Yeah= | R gives feedback. |
| I | =(inaudible) | Not coded. |
| R | (I would say around one pound fifty | R answers (inadequately?). |
| I | Right (pause) over a pound that's a fair a guess. | I gives feedback and ? |

I will now consider some of the findings which emerged from the tape-recording analysis. In Table 1.1, the distribution of actions in questioning by interviewers is given. In all, 2,851 Q-A sequences occurred of which proportionally most were contributed by Interviewer Three.

Table 1.1: Distribution of Actions in Questioning by Interviewers

| Inter-viewer | Question asked as worded or with slight change | | Question significantly altered | | Question completely altered | | Question asked as directive probe | | Question omitted by mistake | | Appropriate card not used | | Number of actual Q-A sequences |
|---|---|---|---|---|---|---|---|---|---|---|---|---|---|
| | n | $\%^a$ | n | $\%^a$ | n | $\%^a$ | n | $\%^a$ | n | $\%^b$ | n | $\%^c$ | n |
| $I_1$ | 170 | 39.72 | 180 | 42.06 | 3 | 0.7 | 50 | 11.68 | 43 | 9.13 | 105 | 52.76 | 428 (9)[d] |
| $I_2$ | 111 | 33.23 | 110 | 29.49 | 5 | 1.5 | 32 | 9.58 | 39 | 10.46 | 117 | 71.34 | 334 (8) |
| $I_3$ | 609 | 72.5 | 30 | 3.57 | 4 | 0.48 | 16 | 1.9 | 16 | 1.87 | 174 | 49.43 | 840 (17) |
| $I_4$ | 338 | 74.29 | 14 | 3.08 | 15 | 3.3 | 6 | 1.32 | 22 | 4.61 | 80 | 39.02 | 455 (10) |
| $I_5$ | 239 | 63.4 | 14 | 3.71 | 1 | 0.27 | 13 | 3.45 | 8 | 2.08 | 103 | 59.54 | 377 (8) |
| $I_6$ | 317 | 76.02 | 22 | 5.28 | 3 | 0.72 | 11 | 2.64 | 23 | 5.23 | 68 | 15.45 | 417 (8) |
| Total | 1784 | 62.57 | 370 | 12.98 | 31 | 1.09 | 128 | 4.49 | 151 | 5.03 | 647 | 51.19 | 2851 (60) |

a.   Computation based on number of actual Q-A sequences.
b.   Computation based on number of possible Q-A sequences.
c.   Only Q-A sequences involving cards considered.
d.   Number of interviews.

It is interesting to note that of all Q-A sequences only 1,784 (or 62.57 per cent) involved the questions being asked as required or with slight change. As regards the correct asking of questions, as with other issues, there are considerable inter-interviewer differences. Interviewer Six (with 76.02 per cent of all her questions asked as required) was best, followed by Interviewers Four (with 74.29 per cent) and Three (with 72.5 per cent). Interviewer Five (with 63.4 per cent) performed less satisfactorily, and Interviewers One (with 39.72 per cent) and Two (33.23 per cent) were worst in the adequate use of the questions. Of all questions asked, 12.98 per cent were significantly altered. This was particularly frequently done by Interviewers One (42.06 per cent of all her questions) and Two (29.49 per cent), while the other interviewers managed much better than average. Questions were completely altered only quite rarely (in 1.09 per cent of all Q-A sequences). Most of such complete alterations were contributed by Interviewer Four (15 out of 31 instances in all). Questions were in 4.49 per cent of all Q-A sequences asked as directive probes. While Interviewers One (with 11.68 per cent of all her sequences) and Two (with 9.58 per cent) are here well above average, Interviewers Three (1.9 per cent) and Four (1.32 per cent) are well below. In all, 5.03 per cent of all questions to be asked were omitted by mistake. This was done least frequently by Interviewers Three (1.87 per cent of all her questions) and Five (2.08 per cent) and most frequently by Interviewers One (9.13 per cent) and Two (10.46 per cent). As regards questions involving the use of cards, roughly every second of such questions (51.19 per cent) was employed differently. Only Interviewer Six (15.45 per cent omissions of the appropriate card) performed here reasonably well.

The consideration of question-asking actions above revealed considerable differences, in terms of rule-following and rule-breaching, between interviewers. Such differences also appear in Table 1.2 where the distribution of probing actions by interviewers is given. In all, 2,278 probes were used (on average 0.8 probe per Q-A sequence) of which only 44.34 per cent (including repetitions of the question) were adequate. As regards adequate probing, Interviewers Three (64.65 per cent of all her probes adequate), Five (58.59 per cent) and Six (54.74 per cent) managed roughly two-thirds of all her probes as required, while Interviewers One (34.83 per cent), Four (27.79 per cent) and Two (21.86 per cent) performed much worse. Of the rule-breaching kinds of probing, inadequate probing (with 20.68 per cent of all probes) and probing unrelated to task (20.46 per cent) were most common followed by directive probing based on R's information (10.1 per cent) and directive

Table 1.2: Distribution of Probing Actions by Interviewers

| Interviewer | Adequate probing | | I repeats the question | | Inadequate probing | | Directive probing based on R's information | | Directive probing based on I's inference | | Probing unrelated to task | | Number of probes used | Mean number of probes used |
|---|---|---|---|---|---|---|---|---|---|---|---|---|---|---|
| | n | % | n | % | n | % | n | % | n | % | n | % | n | x̄ |
| I₁ | 101 | 34.83 | | | 76 | 26.21 | 37 | 12.76 | 22 | 7.59 | 54 | 18.62 | 290 | 0.68 |
| I₂ | 90 | 21.38 | 2 | 0.48 | 74 | 17.58 | 41 | 9.74 | 26 | 6.18 | 188 | 44.66 | 421 | 1.26 |
| I₃ | 383 | 59.38 | 34 | 5.27 | 104 | 16.12 | 62 | 9.61 | 31 | 4.81 | 31 | 4.81 | 645 | 0.77 |
| I₄ | 113 | 26.84 | 4 | 0.95 | 82 | 19.48 | 41 | 9.74 | 16 | 3.8 | 165 | 39.19 | 421 | 0.93 |
| I₅ | 130 | 57.27 | 3 | 1.32 | 64 | 28.19 | 24 | 10.57 | 1 | 0.44 | 5 | 2.2 | 227 | 0.6 |
| I₆ | 127 | 46.35 | 23 | 8.39 | 71 | 25.91 | 25 | 9.12 | 5 | 1.82 | 23 | 8.39 | 274 | 0.66 |
| Total | 944 | 41.44 | 66 | 2.9 | 471 | 20.68 | 230 | 10.1 | 101 | 4.43 | 466 | 20.46 | 2278 | 0.8 |

probing based on the interviewer's inference (4.43 per cent). Besides adequate probing, it was inadequate probing which was most frequently used by all interviewers, with the exception of Interviewers Two and Four whose probing actions involved 44.66 per cent and 39.19 per cent probing unrelated to the task at hand, this accounting, to a large extent, for their high average number of probes used per Q-A sequence (1.26 and 0.93 respectively). Probing unrelated to the task was also quite frequently done by Interviewers One (18.62 per cent of all her probes) and Six (8.39 per cent). Whilst there are hardly any inter-interviewer differences in the extent to which directive probing based on R's information was used, directive probing based on the interviewer's inference was employed more frequently than average by Interviewers One (7.59 per cent of all her probes) and Two (6.18 per cent) and least frequently by Interviewers Six (1.82 per cent) and Five (0.44 per cent).

The distribution of the most relevant respondent actions by interviewers is given in Table 1.3. In all, 7,018 respondent actions are considered, and of these, interestingly, just 43.79 per cent relate to the provision of adequate answers, while 31.55 per cent refer to the provision of inadequate information, 11.98 per cent to feedback, 9.62 per cent to the provision of irrelevant information and 3.06 per cent to requests for clarification. The distribution of respondent actions for each interviewer interacts, of course, with the kinds of questioning and other actions employed by the interviewers. For example, as Interviewers Two and Four were most active in probing for irrelevant information, their respondents (14.88 per cent and 20.29 per cent, respectively, of all the respondents' actions) provided such information much more frequently than average. This is also reflected in their higher than average number of average respondent actions per Q-A sequence (3.18 and 3.15 respectively, as against the average of 2.46 respondent actions). While there is little variation among the interviewers in the frequency of requests for clarification made by respondents, there are some notable differences between interviewers as regards other respondent actions. While roughly two-thirds of all respondent actions for Interviewers Five and Six (58.45 per cent and 55.82 per cent respectively) were related to the provision of adequate answers, only roughly one-third of the respondent actions for Interviewers Two and Four (28.15 per cent and 34.66 per cent respectively) involved this action. As regards the respondents' provision of inadequate information, this occurred much more frequently than average with Interviewer Two (40.58 per cent of all respondent actions), while Interviewer Six encountered such action (24.37 per cent) least. Respondent feedback

Table 1.3: Distribution of Respondent Actions by Interviewers

| Inter-viewer | R answers adequately | | R's information is inadequate | | R's information is irrelevant to the task | | R gives feedback | | R requests clarification | | Number of R's actions | Mean number of R's actions |
|---|---|---|---|---|---|---|---|---|---|---|---|---|
| | n | % | n | % | n | % | n | % | n | % | n | $\bar{x}$ |
| $I_1$ | 437 | 43.74 | 357 | 35.74 | 98 | 9.81 | 82 | 8.21 | 25 | 2.5 | 999 | 2.33 |
| $I_2$ | 299 | 28.15 | 431 | 40.58 | 158 | 14.88 | 138 | 12.99 | 36 | 3.39 | 1062 | 3.18 |
| $I_3$ | 998 | 48.8 | 598 | 29.24 | 94 | 4.6 | 289 | 14.13 | 66 | 3.23 | 2045 | 2.43 |
| $I_4$ | 497 | 34.66 | 430 | 29.99 | 291 | 20.29 | 182 | 12.69 | 34 | 2.37 | 1434 | 3.15 |
| $I_5$ | 377 | 58.45 | 195 | 30.23 | 7 | 1.09 | 44 | 6.82 | 22 | 3.41 | 645 | 1.71 |
| $I_6$ | 465 | 55.82 | 203 | 24.37 | 27 | 3.24 | 106 | 12.73 | 32 | 3.84 | 833 | 2.0 |
| Total | 3073 | 43.79 | 2214 | 31.55 | 675 | 9.62 | 841 | 11.98 | 215 | 3.06 | 7018 | 2.46 |

Table 1.4: Interviewer actions in Answering by Interviewers

| Interviewer | I repeats R's information | | I gives feedback | | I answers for R | | I clarifies adequately | | I clarifies inadequately | | I gives unrelated information | | Probing actions | | Number of I's actions | Mean number of I's actions |
|---|---|---|---|---|---|---|---|---|---|---|---|---|---|---|---|---|
| | n | % | n | % | n | % | n | % | n | % | n | % | n | % | n | $\bar{x}$ |
| $I_1$ | 63 | 9.24 | 260 | 38.12 | 23 | 3.37 | 17 | 2.49 | 11 | 1.61 | 18 | 2.64 | 290 | 42.52 | 682 | 1.59 |
| $I_2$ | 90 | 8.1 | 423 | 38.07 | 58 | 5.22 | 41 | 3.69 | 2 | 0.18 | 76 | 6.84 | 421 | 37.89 | 1111 | 3.33 |
| $I_3$ | 723 | 39.66 | 289 | 15.85 | 71 | 3.89 | 85 | 4.66 | 6 | 0.33 | 4 | 0.22 | 645 | 35.38 | 1823 | 2.17 |
| $I_4$ | 132 | 9.84 | 613 | 45.71 | 43 | 3.21 | 40 | 2.98 | 3 | 0.22 | 89 | 6.64 | 421 | 31.39 | 1341 | 2.95 |
| $I_5$ | 157 | 29.07 | 100 | 18.52 | 32 | 5.93 | 24 | 4.44 | | | | | 227 | 42.04 | 540 | 1.43 |
| $I_6$ | 203 | 27.43 | 178 | 24.05 | 40 | 5.41 | 37 | 5.0 | 1 | 0.14 | 7 | 0.95 | 274 | 37.03 | 740 | 1.77 |
| Total | 1368 | 21.93 | 1863 | 29.87 | 267 | 4.28 | 244 | 3.91 | 23 | 0.37 | 194 | 3.11 | 2278 | 36.52 | 6237 | 2.19 |

was given more frequently than average with Interviewer Three (14.13 per cent of all respondent actions), and was observed to be much below average with Interviewer Five (6.82 per cent). Finally, the particularly low level of actions related to the provision of irrelevant information is noteworthy with Interviewer Five (1.09 per cent of all respondent actions).

The distribution of relevant interviewer actions in answering, that is, after the question has been put to the respondent, by interviewers is given in Table 1.4. In all, 6,237 actions are considered of which most refer to probing (36.52 per cent), followed by the interviewers giving feedback (29.87 per cent), the interviewers repeating information just provided by respondents (21.93 per cent), the interviewers answering for the respondents (4.28 per cent), adequate clarifications (4.28 per cent) and inadequate clarifications (0.37 per cent). Turning to clarifications first, these were mostly performed adequately, with the notable exception of Interviewer One whose clarifications were frequently inadequate (39.29 per cent of all her clarifications). Answering for the respondents, rather than having the respondents answer themselves, was done quite often, although least frequently by Interviewers Four and One (3.21 per cent and 3.37 per cent, respectively, of all their actions). Interviewers Four, One and Two gave feedback much more frequently than average (45.71 per cent, 38.12 per cent and 38.07 per cent, respectively, of all their actions), while, conversely, Interviewers Three, Six and Five employed repeating the respondents' information more frequently than average (39.66 per cent, 29.07 per cent and 27.43 per cent respectively). In all, Interviewers Two and Four interacted most actively with respondents (on average 3.33 and 2.95 actions, respectively, per Q-A sequence), whereas Interviewers One and Five were least active (on average 1.59 and 1.43 actions respectively).

As the tape-recording analysis involved action-by-action coding, various forms of sequence analysis are possible with the data obtained. For reasons of space, I can only give an illustration of this dynamic approach to conversation analysis here, using just tree analysis. In Figure 1.1, a tree representation of the action structure related to the interviewers' correct application of questions requiring the use of prompt cards is given. Such questions, in this survey, had the form of 'How satisfied are you with the size of your house?' requiring the respondents to choose one of a range of predetermined answers listed on a card such as 'Very satisfied, satisfied, between satisfied and dissatisfied, dissatisfied, very dissatisfied'. When such questions were asked as required, in the majority of instances, perhaps after some initial

Figure 1.1: Tree Analysis of Q-A Sequences Involving the Correct Use of Cards (F of transitions n < 5 not considered)

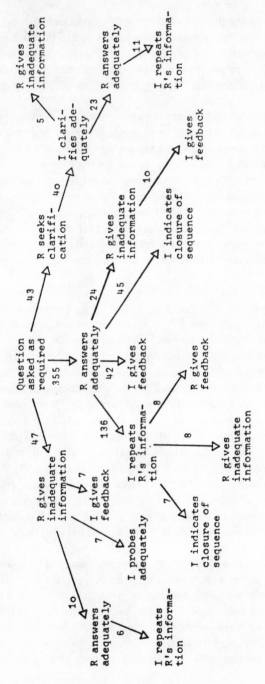

Number of Sequences N = 504

clarification, respondents answered adequately (in 75 per cent of all sequences). Only in 9.33 per cent of all sequences did the respondents provide inadequate information after the question was put to them, which was immediately followed by adequate answering in 21.28 per cent of such sequences. The fact that the question was used correctly and was followed most of the time by adequate answers accounts for the very low volume of probing required (1.38 per cent of all sequences). It is perhaps worth noting, finally, that there are three common interviewer actions following the respondents' provision of adequate answers, these being in 39.43 per cent of the Q-A sequences concerned the interviewer repeating the respondent's information, in 11.6 per cent the interviewer indicating the closure of the sequence by means of saying 'Right' and in 10.82 per cent the interviewer giving feedback.

I will now turn to a tree analysis of Q-A sequences involving the same kind of questions as considered above, except that the card was omitted when the question was first put to the respondent. As indicated in Figure 1.2, in contrast to the correct employment of questions involving cards, omitting the card by mistake leads, after initial clarification where necessary, in the majority (85.08 per cent) of such Q-A sequences to the respondents' provision of inadequate information. In principle, when the card is omitted by mistake, this should involve a repair in the form of using the card as a probe after the occurrence of an inadequate answer. This might be done thus:

| Action | Action Description |
|---|---|
| I Now how satisfied are you with the size of your house? | I asks question as required but fails to use card. |
| R Oh very good. | R gives inadequate information. |
| I Can you look at this card please and give me an answer from there? | I probes adequately. |
| R I'd say satisfied. | R answers adequately. |
| I You're satisfied? | I repeats R's information. |
| R Yes. | R gives feedback. |

In this survey, however, this repair was only employed in 23.93 per cent of the relevant Q-A sequences, although it proved to be immediately effective in 67.33 per cent of all sequences involving adequate probing as remedy. Instead, as response to the respondents' provision of inadequate information, the interviewers used in 18.95 per cent of the relevant Q-A sequences inadequate probing which led in 70 per cent of instances to adequate answers, under the constraint, however, that the full range of answers was not made available to the respondents, this surely giving rise to some response bias. In 9.24 per cent of the

Figure 1.2: Tree Analysis of Q-A Sequences where the Card was Omitted by Mistake (F of transitions n < 5 not considered)

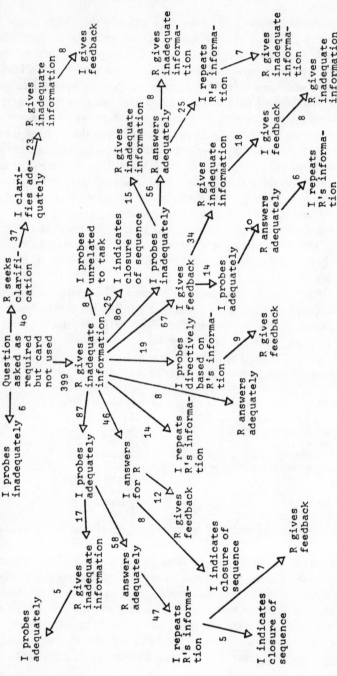

Number of Sequences N = 496

relevant sequences the inadequate information provided was just accepted, either by the interviewers repeating such information or indicating the closure of the sequence. In 10.9 per cent the interviewers acted similarly by just answering for the respondent instead of further probing effort. Directive probing based on R's information was, in contrast to inadequate probing, used quite rarely, that is, in 4.5 per cent of the relevant sequences. The interviewers often gave feedback following the first provision of inadequate information (in 17.77 per cent of all such sequences). This was, however, in 18.67 per cent of these sequences followed by the adequate repair action of adequate probing.


## 4. Conclusion

The kind of conversation analysis favoured in this paper has a number of interesting properties if contrasted with other approaches to the study of conversations (see, for example, Coulthard 1977; Schenkein 1978). First, it requires the researcher to understand, and to conceptualise, conversations in terms of **social situations**. That is to say, conversation analysis, in this view, must explicitly consider the social interactional nature of talk, it being constrained by social rules, role performances and tasks. Secondly, it requires the investigation of a large number of relevant conversations, this providing systematic, rather than just qualitative, insight into the variable forms of social organisation lived and constructed by people in their speech.

Given that conversations are seen here as involving social situations and are studied also quantitatively, the findings thus generated may be useful in a number of ways. First, such conversation analysis contributes to our understanding of social situations in general, beyond mere conversation analysis. Secondly, it is possible to interfere in a sociotechnical sense with aspects of the action structure employed in conversations, if this should be desirable. For example, as regards many of the actions performed by the interviewers discussed above, these were inadequate, and it is possible, using insight into such happenings, to *design* more appropriate action structures in which interviewers might be trained in order to improve their performances (see Brenner 1980).


## References

Austin, J.L. (1975) *How to Do Things with Words*, 2nd edn Clarendon Press, Oxford.

Brenner, M. (1978) 'Interviewing: The Social Phenomenology of a Research Instrument', in M. Brenner, P. Marsh and M. Brenner (eds.) *The Social Contexts of Method*, Croom Helm, London

—— (1980), 'Skills in the Research Interview', in M. Argyle (ed.) *The Handbook of Social Skills*, Methuen, London

Cannell, Ch. F. and Kahn, R.F. (1968) 'Interviewing', in G. Lindzey and E. Aronson (eds.), *The Handbook of Social Psychology*, vol. 2, Addison-Wesley, Reading, Mass.

Coulthard, M. (1977) *An Introduction to Discourse Analysis*, Longman, London

Hyman, H.H. *et al.* (1954) *Interviewing in Social Research*, University of Chicago Press, Chicago

Marquis, K.H. (1967) *Effects of a Household Interview Technique Based on Social Reinforcement*, unpublished PhD thesis, Institute for Social Research, University of Michigan

—— and Cannell, Ch. F. (1969) *A Study of Interviewer-Respondent Interaction in the Urban Employment Survey*, Institute for Social Research, Ann Arbor, Michigan

—— —— (1971) *Effect of Some Experimental Interviewing Techniques on Reporting in the Health Interview Survey* U.S. Department of Health, Education and Welfare, Washington, D.C.

Schenkein, J. (ed) (1978) *Studies in the Organization of Conversational Interaction* Academic Press, London

Smith, J.M. (1972) *Interviewing in Social and Market Research*, Routledge & Kegan Paul, London

Sudman, S. and Bradburn, N.M. (1974) *Response Effects in Surveys*, Aldine, Chicago

# 2 INSTRUMENTALITY SELECTION IN NATURALLY-OCCURRING CONVERSATION: A RESEARCH AGENDA*

Allen D. Grimshaw

## 1. The Problem

Human social actors spend much of their time with others engaged in talk. Given the fundamentally complementary character of social life and its matching of power with weakness, resources with needs, and assertiveness with acquiesence, much of this talk is in some sense manipulative, with speakers attempting to cause (influence) their hearers to alter their behaviours (including speech) or beliefs (or attitudes: for example, experience enhanced or diminished respect for themselves or others) in some way. A general formulation of this phenomenon is:

$$(1) \text{ SOURCE INSTRUMENTALITY GOAL} \left\{ \frac{\text{to}}{\text{into}} \right\} \text{RESULT}$$

where SOURCE is the initial speaker and originator of a manipulative attempt, GOAL the hearer and object of the manipulative attempt, INSTRUMENTALITY a speech act (which may or may not have a verbal label) and RESULT the outcome sought by SOURCE (i.e. an overt behaviour such as provision of goods or a service or utterance or a change in belief or attitudinal disposition of GOAL).[1] While an increasing number of researchers has been investigating the accomplishment of social interaction in ongoing talk, attention to the behavioural repertoires I am labelling INSTRUMENTALITIES has been modest.[2] This is not remarkable; the behaviours are both (i) ubiquitous and therefore 'taken-for-granted',[3] and (ii) extremely complex and resistant to analysis. This paper is a brief discussion of my own contribution to a collaborative project in which such analysis is being attempted.

## 2. A Research Agenda

Most manipulative attempts are made in the course of talk; many utterances directed toward manipulating others (in the restricted sense I use here) are neither direct nor obvious.[4] There is, none the less, a very

41

large number of INSTRUMENTALITIES for which English has specific labels, as well as a substantial number of recognisable (and describable) strategies which are not labelled.[5] A number of interesting issues relate to these verbs and the behaviours they designate. A non-exhaustive list (I am not including specifically linguistic issues such as the interesting question of which verbs require infinitival as contrasted to prepositional complements, and the syntactic and semantic implications of this variation) includes the following:

*2.1.* How does SOURCE select a particular INSTRUMENTALITY in seeking desired outcomes (RESULT) in ongoing interaction, or, put somewhat differently, what independent sociological variables constrain selection of INSTRUMENTALITIES (as tactics or strategies) as dependent variables? In still other words, what are *socially appropriate manipulative behaviours*?

'Order' would be a *grammatically acceptable* INSTRUMENTALITY in any sentence which fits the format specified in (1) in which SOURCE and GOAL were living humans who had interactional access and where RESULT was in control of GOAL. Yet, sociological considerations contrain us to star sentences where SOURCE is subordinate, e.g.

(2) *Grimshaw ordered President Carter to resign.

Or, even among equals, RESULT is of great cost, e.g.

(3) *Dick ordered Henry to stop publishing so much.

(Labov and Fanshel, 1977, make a thorough specification of the several conditions on requests. See especially 77 ff. See also J. Searle 1969, and D. Gordon and G. Lakoff 1975).

*2.2.* Under what circumstances do GOALS of different social characteristics (and with different relations to SOURCE(s)) accede to or resist socially appropriate or inappropriate INSTRUMENTALITIES? What are the behavioural manifestations of resistance? Are there socially appropriate and inappropriate modes?

That an utterance is employed as an INSTRUMENTALITY is sometimes known by an audience only after RESULT has been produced. I once witnessed a senior university official almost run from a room and jump into his automobile when his superior observed, in a surprised voice, 'I'm out of gin.' Only when he returned, breathless, some minutes later, bearing gin, did I realise that he had been 'sent' (or was a true toady). In sharp contrast are other instances in which GOAL(s) may variously mishear, deliberately misunderstand,[6] or, understanding, resist INSTRUMENTALITIES. When INSTRUMENTALITY *is* acknowledged and understood, GOAL(s) may accede, refuse, 'put off', etc. doing RESULT, they may or may not mitigate refusals (see, again, Labov and Fanshel).

*2.3.* What effects does the use (successful or not) of one or another INSTRUMENTALITY have on participants in interaction (SOURCE, GOAL, audience) — and on relationships between or among them?

Subordinates may resent being *'ordered'*; friends may feel embarrassed about asking favours; as a witness to the 'gin' incident I felt contempt for both GOAL and SOURCE. It also happens that people can be 'pleased to be asked', and that witnesses can admire the interactional competence of a particularly subtle or tactful SOURCE.

*2.4.* Are there kinesic and/or prosodic elements associated with the several verbal INSTRUMENTALITIES which are considered as being socially appropriate or inappropriate? Can the production of some kinesic and/or prosodic behaviours be seen as generating messages contrary to those in the 'main' verbal channel? What are they? What are responses to them by participants?

Voice quality and kinesic behaviours are heavily implicated in what Hymes (1974:57 ff) has called *'key'*, a combination of speech act elements which can, when 'in conflict with the overt content of an act', override the latter (58). The military, with its emphasis on 'command voice' and 'command bearing' has long been aware of the importance of *key*; parents tell children to apologise 'as if you mean it'.

*2.5.* What are the distinctive grammatical and other features of jointly produced (i.e. by more than one interactant) INSTRUMENTALITIES or responses?

It not infrequently occurs that SOURCE, because of considerations of deference or concern over the propriety of seeking a RESULT, will use an INSTRUMENTALITY which is so indirect that GOAL will be unable to determine what RESULT is being sought. Third parties may then provide metalinguistic glosses, e.g. 'What he is trying to say (ask you for . . .) is . . .' etc. GOAL(s) may, themselves, help in the formulation of an INSTRUMENTALITY. An instance of third-party collaboration appears in the text discussed later in this paper.

*2.6.* What labels (e.g. verb names) are assigned to INSTRUMENTALITIES by competent native speakers or how are they otherwise acceptably identified?[7] Do the variables which constrain selection also constrain the acceptability, to other native speakers, of reports of past or ongoing behaviour? What is the nature of metalinguistic discussion of strategies by interactants (or audiences)?

Minor officials don't '*order*' heads of state to resign, and the latter don't '*wheedle*' their subordinates into showing them official plans — nor would reporters accept reports that such events had, indeed, occurred. Similarly, students would smile at a peer who reported that he/she would '*command*' a teacher to cancel classes for the remainder of term. People spend a considerable amount of time planning (even 'rehearsing', see Goffman 1974) and discussing INSTRUMENTALITIES past and projected.

*2.7.* How are INSTRUMENTALITIES serially employed for the accomplishment (joint or individual) of outcomes superordinate to specific manipulative attempts, i.e. how do the latter 'fit into' episodes and into the larger speech events (e.g. court trials, staff medical sessions, family 'conferences', etc.) of which both INSTRUMENTALITIES and episodes are constituents?

This is the question of 'discourse levels' which led Sinclair and Coulthard (1975) to posit the increasingly comprehensive elements of **act, move, exchange, transaction,** and **lesson.** Similar hierarchies can be elaborated with other speech events (Hymes 1974), e.g. trial, diagnosis, therapy session, collective bargaining session, dissertation defense, or whatever, at the top level.

Each of these seven questions is being addressed by one or another of the participants in the collaborative research of which my own work on INSTRUMENTALITIES is a part. There are at least two additional, and critical, issues, which cannot be investigated with our data:

*2.8.* How are these verbal (and other) manipulative skills acquired? Are there developmental stages in acquisition? Are these skills equivalently acquired by all native speakers of a language?

It appears that these complex skills in discourse are acquired in the same developmental manner as language itself is acquired (see, for example, Bates 1976; Cook-Gumperz and Corsaro 1977; Corsaro 1979; and articles in Mitchell-Kernan and Ervin-Tripp 1977 and Goody 1978) and that performance skills are unequally distributed within speech communities (see, for example, Albert 1974 and Grimshaw and Holden 1976).

*2.9.* Can the several INSTRUMENTALITIES be mapped into a bounded multi-dimensional space? Are the dimensions the same as the sociological constraints on strategy selection? How are locations of coordinates to be plotted (i.e. how are the sociological variables to be measured!)?

These questions are only adumbrated in the extant literature. For a preliminary formulation of the conceptual issue and identification of some first steps toward measurement, see Grimshaw (1980a) and sources cited therein.


## 3. The Project

Scholarly investigation of naturally occurring talk is a quite recent phenomenon which has rapidly captured the attention of a very large number of researchers. Anthropologists, linguists, philosophers, psychologists, and sociologists have all become interested in social accomplishment through talk; they have collectively studied events including, nonexhaustively, telephone conversations, therapy sessions, labour-management bargaining, classroom interaction, shamanistic curing sessions, religious rituals, greeting exchanges, and litigation, in literally dozens of different societies and speech communities. Data have been drawn from observational and experimental studies and have been variously overtly and covertly recorded using a variety of sorts of equipment. This diversity of disciplinary perspectives, substantive foci, and methods of data collection and analysis has provided interested students with a wealth of knowledge about speech events in a variety of cultures and settings within those varied cultures, with a rich conceptual apparatus, and even with some notions about possible universals. This same richness and diversity, however, has concomitant costs. Most particularly, there have been few instances in which different theoretical perspectives and/or analytic modes have been brought to bear on identical speech events (or, for that matter, in any systematic way on similar events in different speech communities). Consequently, the growth of a cumulative base of shared understanding about talk has been considerably slower than that of the literature as a whole.

Collaterally, the research studies and theoretical developments just alluded to have done little to date to test the relative *power* of analytic approaches or to isolate exactly which elements or aspects of discourse, natural conversation and verbal interaction are most crucial to each mode of analysis. The Multiple Analysis Project (MAP) is posited on the belief that the time is ripe to pose such questions and to ask that the several analytic perspectives be made more explicit so that they can be compared, tested against each other, and made mutually accessible.

The MAP believes, moreover, that this can best be done by having research scholars representing several emergent theoretical and methodological perspectives analyse a common corpus of data or 'text'. To this end a number of scholar researchers representing the several disciplines listed above (with the exception of philosophy) and a variety of theoretical and methodological perspectives have joined in a joint enterprise in which they have agreed, individually and in teams, to analyse a common record of a naturally occurring speech event.[8]

## 4. The Data

The event being analysed is a doctoral dissertation defence;[9] all MAP participants will do analyses based on the record of a ten-minute segment of the defence which includes the end of the committee's *in camera* deliberations, the period in which the supervisor has left the room to bring back the candidate, and the beginning of the period after the candidate's return. The defence was selected for recording and analysis because it met several theoretical and technical criteria. Most important among the former were (i) 'salience'[10] for participants (a defence is, in spite of its 'ritual' character, a critical career juncture in which participants have sharply discrepant power), and (ii) density of interaction (there are variously four, three, and five interactants in the common segment).[11] The defence was scheduled for a room in which light and sound levels could be controlled and in which seating arrangements permitted an optimally complete visual record (including full bodies of participants, an important consideration for colleagues doing kinesic analyses).[12]

### 4.1 The Data Record

The data record includes frame-numbered colour film footage (about one hour of the two-hour defence, almost continuous for the ten minute segment), reel-to-reel stereo audio (continuous throughout except for tape changes), monaural cassettes (for use with the Varispeech 'sound stretcher'), a variety of transcripts (including a detailed transcript employing the notational conventions developed by Gail Jefferson for the common segment), still photographs of the interactants, modest biographical information on interactants, and a modest ethnographic record of events leading up to the defence itself.[13]

## 5. Analytic Procedures

Each of the several MAP analysts (or analyst teams) is employing procedures specific to the questions they are asking. In my work on manipulation I am employing an adaptation of the frame developed by Labov and Fanshel (1977) in their pioneering study of therapeutic discourse. Labov and Fanshel distinguish eight analytic procedures they employed once they had their data in hand: (i) editing (a continuous process throughout the course of research on discourse occurring 'live'); (ii) identification of fields of discourse (e.g. Everyday style as contrasted to Formal or Interview); (iii) investigation of paralinguistic cues (ranging, in my work, from intonation and hesitation to pronominal usage and, for example, selection of deictic markers); (iv) expansion (i.e. what is *actually* being said, see 5.2.1); (v) specification of propositions (recurrent assertions about the 'world' or about specific actors in an ongoing interactional event, i.e. 'Discourse analysis is difficult' or 'The candidate has done a good job', respectively); (vi) discovery of discourse rules (e.g. in Labov and Fanshel, admitting or challenging presuppositions, making or putting off requests, etc.); (vii) analysis of interaction (i.e. what gets done with what gets said, see 5.2.2); and (viii) explication of sequential order (a concern more central to other MAP analysts).[14] My analysis is in some ways a test of their procedures in a different type of conversational event; it differs in: (a) the nature of the event studied, (b) the number of participants, (c) my emphasis on INSTRUMENTALITIES (though they are much concerned with manipulative behaviour), and (d) my use of the visual record available in the MAP data set.

### 5.1 A Draft Specimen Analysis

The appendix is in three parts. The first provides a short characterisation of the cast of characters and, synoptically and unfortunately somewhat cryptically, a chronicle of the defence up to the time at which the test displayed began. The subsequent section incorporates a summary of immediately following conversation and a description of the rest of the defence. The rest of the appendix is a specimen draft analysis, consisting of the text of the initial 25 seconds of the 1.5 minutes in the first of the nine episodes into which I have divided the segment,[15] along with my notes on paralinguistic and kinesic features of participant utterances and initial expansions and characterisations of what is being done interactionally. The fragment has been chosen for display because it includes, among other things, instances of: (i) use of an indirect

INSTRUMENTALITY in (ii) an apparently unsuccessful communicative (manipulative) act, followed by (iii) third party intervention in a variety of 'remedial work' (Goffman 1971) and (iv) joint construction of a somewhat less inferentially demanding INSTRUMENTALITY.

Other analysts might not agree with my characterisation of and comments on paralinguistic and kinesic cues and other analysts *have* disagreed with my expansions and interpretations of interactional moves.[16] This lack of consensus notwithstanding, I think that what I have attempted to do should be fairly clear. The draft analysis does not include full specification of propositions (some of which will probably drop out at later states of the analysis), nor explication of sequential order (which is being examined by others). As limitations of space make it impossible for me to go over even this short fragment in detail, I will say something here about expansions and analyses of interaction. I hope that my necessarily truncated comments will make it possible for readers to retrieve unexplicated procedures from the draft.

*5.2.1. Expansion.* Expansion aims at synthetic integration of a variety of sources of information into an elaboration of what is 'actually' being *said* (in contrast to what is being *done*, see analysis of interaction, 5.2.2).

It incorporates not only verbal text and paralinguistic and kinesic cues, but also an explication of forward and backward reference (in the Halliday-Hasan 1976 sense of 'textual cohesion') and shared knowledge of participants. It aims, in other words, *to reproduce participants' procedures in everyday conversation*. Thus, for example, a partial expansion of A's first utterance:

(4) .h So *you* say *pass:*.

might look something like the following:

> You have not announced your *relative* evaluation of the dissertation or the candidate's performance in the defence. Candidates have a right to know the content of such evaluations – committee members have obligations to provide them. Failure to make a positive evaluation can be interpreted as making a negative one. I am giving you an opportunity (inviting you, pushing you) to be more specific . . .

A more familiar instance from everyday life might be the expansion of a spouse's (or parent's or employer's) utterance:

(5) Well, what happened *this* time?

as:

You are late again and this is a topic on which I have previously expressed disgruntlement. You have obligations to meet here and at the very least you should inform me when you are not going to meet those obligations. You frequently claim conflicting obligations. I suppose that you will this time. I am sceptical.

Such expansions may be extended, revised, or even rejected as additional materials in a corpus are examined and incorporated. A different topic referred to by the 'well' in the second utterance, for example, someone's continuing attempts to obtain some end from a third party, would engender a different expansion. The analytic processes, however, remain the same.

*5.2.2. Analysis of interaction.* Concern with what is being *done*, namely, 'challenges, defenses and retreats, which have to do with *the status of participants, their rights and obligations, and their changing relationships in terms of social organization*' (Labov and Fanshel 1977: 58-9, emphasis added), is both the central focus of discourse analysis and its sociological endpoint.[17] Like Labov and Fanshel, I am interested in specifying the ways in which interactants act to interpret what goes on in verbal interaction. In the first example above, this means determining how participants can interpret a 'simple' comment such as 'So *you* say *pass*' as simultaneously **requesting** that GOAL *provide* a more detailed evaluation and subtly **criticising** the addressee as having been remiss in meeting a professional obligation. In the second, it means determining how participants can interpret an utterance in question form not as a question but rather as a complaint, or an accusation, or an attribution of negative qualities, or possibly an invitation to disputation. Labov and Fanshel list some 56 interactional 'terms' in their index; the several varieties of behaviour are not mutually exclusive. I also have a lengthy list, which will be changed many times before the analysis is in anything like a final form. The fact of the matter is, however, that it *is* interaction that gets accomplished in conversation, and the kind of analysis published by Labov and Fanshel and being attempted in my work does provide a systematic mapping of the route followed to arrive at a characterisation of what it is that participants are *doing*.

## 6. Conversation Analysis and Sociological Theory

I am not a linguist, my interests are not in the structure of conversation but rather in how *social* structure is constructed through interaction and manifested in discourse. I believe that conversational records like the one we are jointly analysing constitute a particularly useful sociological resource and that careful study of such records is a sociologically profitable enterprise. Ideally, I would like every reader to view the MAP footage and listen to our audio. Ideally, I would like to present a fully explicated analysis of an extensive corpus of text. The data record is not yet available for distribution (parts of it will be included in the final MAP report) and space limitations will not allow extensive development of a textual analysis.[18] I do hope that some readers will take the time to follow through the draft specimen analysis which has been provided (keeping in mind the qualification that it will probably be considerably changed by the time analysis is completed).

It is possible, however, to at least identify some of the sociologically relevant findings to which my research is leading. I will try to do this first by saying something about kinds of nonsuccesses in communicative (manipulative and otherwise) attempts and secondly by discussing some social variables which have effects both on INSTRUMENTALITY selection and reporting and on the social distribution of successful and nonsuccessful communicative attempts.

## 6.1 A Taxonomy of Outcomes of Communicative Events

Whatever interpretation may be made of A's intentions and INSTRUMENTALITY selection in his opening utterance in the appended text, it seems clear that that INSTRUMENTALITY was not successful in causing J to produce the behaviour sought by A. I have argued in another place (Grimshaw 1980b) that several, quite different and analytically distinct outcomes are possible when S makes an utterance with the primary intention that H do (believe) r (RESULT in the convention here employed).

It is at least heuristically useful to distinguish among utterances as being, variously: (i) **nonheard** (signal inaudible or undecipherable); (ii) **understood as intended** (the modal case, in which RESULT may or may not follow depending upon fulfilment of various 'preconditions' (on which see, for example, Searle 1969; Gordon and Lakoff 1975; Labov and Fanshel 1977) and in which, further, nonRESULT will be accompanied or accomplished by e.g. challenge, denial, inaction, refusal, etc.); (iii) **nonunderstood or partially or ambiguously understood** (unambiguous signal and acceptance of Cooperative Principle (Grice 1975) in conjunction with non-shared understandings of expectations and/or contexts. Hearers are frequently aware of nonsuccess in such instances, and may make clarification requests; they may also rely on Cicourel's (1974) 'retrospective-prospective sense of occurrence' and other interpretive procedures to 'recover' what they have missed); (iv) **misheard** (mishearings occur where there is an unambiguous signal and acceptance of the Cooperative Principle *and* where H is confident that she/he has correctly heard and understood S's utterance and has the linguistic capacity to have done so in the absence of mishearing), and (v) **misunderstood**.

I define misunderstanding as a two-stage process in which H experiences understanding and then deliberately fails to acknowledge that experiencing. Misunderstandings vary along at least three continua: (a) overtness-covertness, i.e. they may be blatant and obviously intended, recoverable but ambiguous (S may suspect having been 'had', but not be sure) or well-concealed – and these variations themselves be intended or not by H; (b) friendliness-unfriendliness, i.e. they may be whimsical, teasing, or punitive or altruistic, self-protective, embarrassing, or outright malicious; (c) excusability-justifiability, i.e. if H is 'caught in the act' or accused of wilful misinterpretation he/she will be able to justify, excuse, mitigate, apologise (or not) for the violation of the Cooperative Principle.[19]

I will argue, shortly, that both S's perception and evaluation of the nature of communicative nonsuccess and S's reaction (as well as the perceptions, evaluations, and reactions of observers) will be constrained by the same set of social variables which constrain S's choice of INSTRUMENTALITY and observer reports of INSTRUMENTALITIES employed, i.e. power, affect, and cost (or utility).

## 6.2 The Principal Dimensions

Power, affect and utility are central notions in the conceptual armoraria of political science and sociology, sociological and psychological social psychology, and economics, respectively; it is not surprising that they insistently emerge as critical considerations in the study of social accomplishment in naturally occurring conversation. I have found, both in my analysis of the dissertation defense and in other work (on verbal strategies and on nonsuccesses in communication) that Speaker, Hearer, and Observer behaviours and perceptions of those of others are constrained by relationships of power and affect *between* SOURCE and GOAL (with additional effects introduced by the same relationships with audiences) and by RESULT's cost for GOAL and salience for SOURCE (the latter two can be combined into a variable of utility). The use of these several dimensions in largely intuitive exploratory analyses of the text more formally addressed in the appendix of this paper and of a 'script' involving known public figures (Grimshaw 1980a) permitted me to make a number of specific observations, such as:

(A) Efforts to manipulate are most likely when RESULT has high **valence** for both SOURCE and GOAL and where **cost** will be low for both.

(B) Mutual positive affect devalues some INSTRUMENTALITIES.

(C) Mutual negative affect precludes use of some INSTRUMENTALITIES.

(D) Subordinate or equal position of SOURCE precludes use of some INSTRUMENTALITIES.

(E) *Ceteris paribus*, RESULT determines whether an effort will be made.

(F) Hierarchy constrains the range of INSTRUMENTALITIES available.

(G) Within that range interaction of **affect** and **utility** constrain specific selection.

Such formulations are now new in the disciplines named above (see, for example, Heider 1958 and the derivative literatures in attribution and exchange theories); their explanatory usefulness in studies of talk has been less widely acknowledged. Stated in sometimes quite similar ways, however, propositions like those just listed have been validated by several different investigators using a variety of sociolinguistic data. Brown and Levinson (1978), for example, identify **power, social distance**, and **rank of imposition** (cost) as the critical variables in selection of strategies along the interacting continua of efficiency and politeness. Labov and Fanshel (1977:59) invoke the Brown and Gilman (1960) dimensions of **power** and **solidarity**. Heise (1979) has used the semantic differential in an attempt to measure attributes of **power** and **affect-induction** of specific role positions and associated behaviours (including modes of talk). The convergence is marked — it is not, on reflection, remarkable.

These same three variables, with the addition of S's assessment of H's intentions and the presence or absence of mitigating behaviours by H, are critical, I believe, in determining S responses to unsuccessful communicative attempts. It seems reasonable to expect, for example, that S's possibly negative reactions will be muted when H has greater relative power, when the affectual relationship between S and H is tenuous but valued by S, and when RESULT is 'not worth the fuss'. Contrarywise, powerful Ss are less constrained to respond cautiously. It further seems reasonable to expect that, for example, mishearings resulting from H's defects of skill (or knowledge) or even of carelessness or lack of attention, are more likely to be charitably seen than what S sees as wilful misunderstandings.

Finally, S's potentially negative emotional response and subsequent behaviours may be ameliorated by mitigating behaviours from H who, having acted in a way that could produce a negative reaction, acts to avoid that outcome by apologising, providing RESULT, attempting to turn the event into a 'joke', or other remedial behaviours.[20] Consideration of the interaction of these several dimensions has permitted me (1980b) to suggest an additional set of propositional relationships. Illustrative of these are:

(H) As H's power relative to S's increases, it is less likely that S will openly attribute nonsuccess to (deliberate) misunderstanding resulting from defects of intention and more likely that S will suppress aggressive reactions;

(I) as the utility assigned by S to RESULT increases, so does the likelihood that S will try to correct possible sources of nonsuccess — the behaviour S chooses will reflect, *inter alia*, considerations of power and affect;

(J) the 'clearer' S believes (perceives) her/his initial utterance (INSTRUMENTALITY) to have been, the more likely that nonsuccess will be attributed to H's defects of improper intention.

Their quasi-formal statement notwithstanding, (A)–(J) are propositional statements or testable hypotheses, not demonstrated discourse rules, propositions, or conversational postulates. They are derived from close examination of naturally occurring conversation like that in the appended text from the MAP corpus. I believe that they make that text more meaningful, in the ordinary sense of that term, in that they make understandable both A's very considerable obliqueness in his initial INSTRUMENTALITY and the circumspection obvious in his follow-up in the wake of his initial nonsuccess. In the case of the latter, for example, each of the last three propositions is given support: (i) J's situational power is high (in that he has available the option of making a negative evaluation, something that A clearly wants to avoid) and A does not attribute nonsuccess to misunderstanding; (ii) the utility assigned RESULT by A is high, he attempts to remedy the nonsuccess, he continues to do so in an oblique manner; (iii) A appears to acknowledge that his initial INSTRUMENTALITY was less than clear, and avoids attribution of nonsuccess to J's defects of intention. The mode of analysis invoked permits specification of what is being *done* interactionally.

Individuals vary in perceptions of hierarchy, affect, cost and so on, power can be situationally specific, and intuitions may vary about what INSTRUMENTALITIES are congruent with what combinations of variable weights. Individuals, moreover, differ in personal styles and emotional volatility, whatever the combinations of the three principal variables, and there is increasing evidence that there are differences in repertoires available to, for example, class, sexual, or occupational categories. None the less, I believe a persuasive case can be made that the kind of perspective sketched in this paper, and the agenda of questions raised in the case of INSTRUMENTALITY selection and alluded to in the brief reference to non-success, provide a useful basis for the sociological investigation of: (a) *the cultural and social knowledge necessary for competence in rules related to sociolinguistic appropriateness*, (b) *what native speakers will accept as semantically appropriate characterisations and labelling of what a S (SOURCE) has done (or is doing – or has available to do) to an H (GOAL) in order to obtain (or attempt to obtain) RESULT*, and (c) *the kinds of considerations involved in S's perceptions of and responses to nonsuccesses in communication.* Further work on the analysis of the dissertation defence will permit a test of this belief.

**Appendix: A Specimen Draft Analysis**

*1. Introduction*

This appendix is divided into three parts. Following this introduction there will be a very brief characterisation of a 'typical dissertation defence', some very superficial sketches of participants in the defence, a statement about the behaviour of the participants in the main part of the defence (i.e. during questioning of the candidate), and a summary description of participant speech acts in the 1.5 minute period between the departure of the candidate and the beginning of the exchange recorded in the specimen text. That text and accompanying analytic comments follow a short second part, containing very brief descriptions of the remainder of the episode from which the text is drawn and of the rest of the defence.

## 2. Antecedent Context

The text fragment is excerpted from a doctoral dissertation defence in a midwestern (USA) sociology department. The defence is much like others in its temporal unfolding, in participant characteristics and in the variety of behaviours displayed.

*2.1 The 'Typical' Defence.* Like most such events, this one was divided into four major sections: (i) **openings**, i.e. 'settling in', statement of procedures, and candidate's statement; (ii) **defence**, i.e. questioning of the candidate followed by brief discussion of publication plans, etc.; (iii) **committee deliberations**, i.e. *in camera* discussion of candidate's graduate career, dissertation project, professional prospects, etc., and the taking of a formal or consensual decision to be reported to the candidate; and (iv) **closings**, i.e. candidate's return, congratulations (however qualified or contingent), bookkeeping, discussion of projected activities, disengagement. The sections vary in length; in most such defences the defence proper takes about half the total time (somewhat more than an hour in this case) with remaining time divided more or less evenly among the other activities.

*2.2 The Cast of Characters.* The candidate, who does not appear in the text following, is a female of forty-plus years. A, J, and S are male full professors of sociology; all are forty or older. A and S have been colleagues for nearly twenty years; J, who is somewhat younger, has been a member of the department for eleven years. A is the candidate's dissertation supervisor. P, also a senior faculty member, is female and a full professor of psychology who has been actively involved in advising the candidate.

A, as supervisor, chaired the questioning period and did not take the floor for systematic questioning of the candidate. His questions were primarily directed to clarification; he also offered interpretations of both questions and answers of other participants. He sometimes defended L's answers or choice of procedures. J, P, and S were each formally given the floor for questioning; all four faculty members made queries and comments when others had the floor. J used the floor to critically question the candidate's methodological procedures and theoretical discussion and to raise issues related to practical (or policy) implications of her work. P also raised questions concerning procedures or interpretations; she also engaged in some defending behaviour. S made a number of comments and suggestions, engaged in some defending behaviour, and tended to ask clarifying questions or questions stimulated by the immediate context of the ongoing discussion. A, P, and S are generally supportive; J is neither supportive nor actively hostile.

*2.3 The Immediately Prior Context.* The 1.5 minutes (actually somewhat longer, a tape change occurs) following the candidate's departure and immediately preceding the displayed text sequentially include: (i) an exchange in which S teases A about difficulty in locating the meeting room; (ii) a 'heavily implicative' (Labov-Fanshel 1977: 47) 'so' by A initiating the business of the closed session; (iii) a request from A to J for reactions; (iv) J's reaction (he lists some problems but concludes, 'I would certainly be in favour of uh, you know *passing her*'); (v) general discussion of the length (a theme of the entire defence) and density of argument of the dissertation; and (vi) a brief narrative by A about a writing project he terminated when one chapter reached 220 pages in length. That narrative is immediately followed by the first utterance in the text following.

## 3. The Specimen

The 25 seconds included in the specimen text and analysis occur at the very beginning of the common MAP corpus and the analytic comments reflect the uncertainties and problematic character of my initial entry into the data. Some revision has already been done, much more will be necessary; analysis of subsequent episodes currently being done looks different. The goal of explicating interactional accomplishment remains unchanged, however, and I do not anticipate that the characterisation of interaction in the specimen will change markedly. The most likely changes are (i) simplification of notation for propositions and interactional moves (and, at some point, a reduction in the number of propositions); and (ii) incorporation of information on kinesic behaviours of not-currently-speaking interactants.

The legend includes only conventions employed in the specimen text.

## 4. And Then What Happened?

During the approximately one minute remaining in the initial episode, J completes the 'elaboration' begun at the end of the displayed text. He does add some evaluation by stating, 'this *project* for *her* has been everything and *more* I think than a dissertation *should* be' at the candidate's '*stage* of . . . professional *development*' and that it is 'a *good* job and she ought to be *commended*'. He also complains, indirectly, however, about the candidate's undeveloped sense of relevance as manifested by the length of the dissertation. To that last, S responds that if she had not looked at everything she did, 'someone on this *committee* would have *said*, should you have *examined*?' J, in turn, responds by referring to the candidate's 'compulsion'.

This exchange is followed by evaluation (positive) from S, further discussion, and a passing positive evaluation from P. At the end of six minutes A leaves the room to bring back the candidate; there is a very brief period of fairly desultory talk among the three persons remaining for about a minute. The remainder of the time (in the common MAP corpus) after the return of A and L is taken up primarily by discussion of earlier reports of sexual discrimination. The final ten minutes of the full data record includes continuation of that last discussion, a review of future plans, the completion of bookkeeping, etc. The record ends as the participants are preparing to leave.

## Analysis

*Legend*

1. The transcription conventions within the text are adaptations of those of Gail Jefferson, as they appear in Sacks, Schegloff and Jefferson (1974).

2. The analytic conventions (adapted from Labov and Fanshel 1977) for propositional moves are:

    $\longleftarrow$ = backward referencing, e.g. reminders, answers;
    $\longrightarrow$ = forward referencing, e.g. proposals, questions;
    $\longleftrightarrow$ = global (non temporally bound) referencing, e.g. claims, challenges.

3. Citation references:
    H-H = Halliday and Hasan, 1976
    L-F = Labov and Fanshel, 1977.

*Text and Analysis*

(1)
A . H SO *YOU* SAY *PASS*.

PC

NO HESITATION. STATEMENT INTONATION, MODEST STRESS ON *YOU* AND *PASS* WITH *PASS* SOMEWHAT 'STRETCHED OUT'. THE CAUSAL SO IS ONE WHICH ALWAYS APPEARS IN INITIAL POSITION (OR FOLLOWING AND) AND IS INTERNAL IN THE SENSE THAT IT REFERS TO SPEAKER'S (A'S, HERE) REASONING PROCESS: 'I CONCLUDE FROM WHAT YOU SAY (OR OTHER EVIDENCE)' – THE EXPRESSION 'I GATHER' COULD BE SUBSTITUTED (H-H 256–7). THERE IS ANOTHER USE OF SO MEANING ESSENTIALLY, 'IT IS THE CASE THAT ...' (H-H 138–9). THE FIRST INTERPRETATION IS MORE PLAUSIBLE HERE. IF IT WERE THE CASE THAT SO WERE STRESSED HERE, IT WOULD CARRY 'HEAVY IMPLICATION' (L-F 47), THEREBY SIGNALLING 'THERE IS MORE TO THIS THAN MEETS THE EYE' (IBID.), POSSIBLY IMPLYING SOMETHING 'WRONG' OR 'QUESTIONABLE'. THE STRESS IS NOT PRESENT AND, AS THE SUBSEQUENT TEXT SHOWS, 'CONVERSATIONAL IMPLICATURE' IS REQUIRED TO DERIVE A READING OF A'S INTENDED MEANING.

KC

CONSIDERABLE BODY READJUSTMENT – ORIENTING TOWARD J IN POSITION WHICH SCHEFLEN HAS CHARACTERISED AS CHALLENGING.

X

YOU HAVE CHARACTERISED THE CANDIDATE'S PERFORMANCE AS 'PASS' – YOU HAVE NOT PROVIDED A *RELATIVE* EVALUATION OF THE DISSERTATION AND OF THE CANDIDATE'S DEFENCE. CANDIDATES HAVE A RIGHT TO KNOW THE CONTENT OF SUCH EVALUATIONS – COMMITTEE MEMBERS HAVE OBLIGATIONS TO PERFORM THEM. I BELIEVE YOU SHOULD PROVIDE A SPECIFICATION OF 'PASS'.

[ALT. X: YOU HAVE CHARACTERISED THE CANDIDATE'S PERFORMANCE AS *PASS* YOU HAVE NOT PROVIDED A *RELATIVE* EVALUATION OF THE DISSERTATION AND OF THE CANDIDATE'S DEFENCE. L IS MY STUDENT, AND SUPERVISORS ARE JUDGED BY HOW WELL THEIR STUDENTS PERFORM. I WOULD LIKE YOU TO SAY THAT SHE DID WELL – SUCH A CHARACTERISATION WILL REDOUND TO MY CREDIT.]

I

A INITIATES THE EPISODE IN INTERVIEW STYLE BY REFERRING TO J'S EARLIER CHARACTERISATION OF L'S PERFORMANCE AND SUGGESTING THAT J HAD FAILED TO PROVIDE AN OBLIGATORY RELATIVE EVALUATION *<nMOE*, THEREBY CHALLENGING *<?MEET>* J'S COMPETENCE.

[ALT. I: A INITIATES THE INTERVIEW IN INTERVIEW STYLE BY REFERRING TO J'S EARLIER CHARACTERISATION OF L'S PERFORMANCE AND SUGGESTING THAT J HAD FAILED TO PROVIDE AN OBLIGATORY RELATIVE EVALUATION *<nMOE*, THEREFORE FAILING TO POSITIVELY EVALUATE A *<n+SESP*. A THEREBY CHALLENGES *<?COLL=⇒>* J'S COLLEGIALITY.

PC

STATEMENT INTONATION

KC

NODS HEAD UP AND DOWN SLIGHTLY DURING UTTERANCE. PUNCTUATES END OF UTTERANCE WITH VERY SLIGHT HAND MOVEMENT.

AKC

CONTINUES TO MOVE FORWARD IN 'CHALLENGING' POSITION. CONSIDERABLE BODY MOVEMENT.

X

I AGREE THAT I SAID 'PASS'.

I

AGREES WITH A.

(2).

J. $\breve{O}H$, YEAH.=

(3)

A. =AND D̈I- ÄH- D̈I- IS *THAT* A: UH,

UH, THAT'S A *NEUTRAL* TERM.
(RASP)

PC
TENSION; HESITATION, SELF-INTERRUPTION, UNEVEN TEMPO. STRESS ON *THAT* AND ON *NEUTRAL*. LAST PHRASE STATE-MENT INTONATION WITHOUT HESITATION.

KC
MAINTAINS 'CHALLENGING' POSITION. UTTERANCE PUNC-TUATED BY CONSIDERABLE GESTICULATION.

X
I AM NOT SURE HOW I SHOULD SAY THIS, SINCE YOU APPAR-ENTLY EITHER DID NOT UNDERSTAND MY LAST UTTERANCE OR HAVE CHOSEN TO ACT AS IF YOU DID NOT. YOU AGREE THAT YOU SAID 'PASS', YOU ACT AS IF YOU BELIEVE THAT TO BE AN ADEQUATE CHARACTERISATION. I AM RELUCTANT TO SUGGEST DIRECTLY THAT YOU HAVE NOT PROVIDED THE *RELATIVE* EVALUATION WHICH IS THE CANDIDATE'S RIGHT TO HAVE AND YOUR OBLIGATION TO PROVIDE. I WILL NOTE AGAIN THAT 'PASS', DOES NOT PROVIDE A RELATIVE TERM BY EMPHASISING THE NEUTRALITY. [ALT. X: I AM NOT SURE HOW I SHOULD SAY THIS, SINCE YOU APPARENTLY EITHER DID NOT UNDERSTAND MY LAST UTTERANCE OR HAVE CHOSEN TO ACT AS IF YOU DID NOT. YOU AGREE THAT YOU SAID *PASS*, YOU ACT AS IF YOU BELIEVE THAT TO BE AN ADEQUATE CHARACTERISATION. I WOULD LIKE YOU TO PROVIDE A MORE POSITIVE CHARACTERISATION, THEREBY COMPLIMENTING ME.]

I
A IS RELUCTANT TO DIRECTLY QUESTION *CRIT>* J AND DEMONSTRATES THIS RELUCTANCE THROUGH MANIFEST DIFFICULTY IN UTTERANCE PRODUCTION. THE UTTERANCE CONCLUDES, HOWEVER, WITH A REMINDER THAT J HAS FAILED TO PROVIDE THE OBLIGATORY RELATIVE EVALU-ATION *<nMOE=J*, THEREBY INDIRECTLY CHALLENGING

<?MEET-J> J'S COMPETENCE AND REQUESTING J TO MAKE A RELATIVE EVALUATION.

[ALT. I:A IS RELUCTANT TO DIRECTLY QUESTION CRIT> AND J DEMONSTRATES THIS RELUCTANCE THROUGH MANIFEST DIFFICULTY IN UTTERANCE PRODUCTION. THE UTTERANCE CONCLUDES, HOWEVER, WITH A REMINDER THAT J HAS FAILED TO PROVIDE A POSITIVE EVALUATION OF A THROUGH PRAISE OF CANDIDATE <n+SESP>, THEREBY CHALLENGING <?COLL> J'S COLLEGIALITY.]

(4)
J. /I'M NOT/SURE.
  ((BREATHY VOICE))
A

A. OVERLAP WITH 5.

PC
QUIET STATEMENT.
KC
SLIGHT HEAD TILT.
X
I DON'T KNOW WHAT YOU ARE TALKING ABOUT.

I
J INDIRECTLY ASSERTS THAT A <nCP-M-A HAS VIOLATED THE MAXIM OF MANNER. HE DOES THIS CIRCUMSPECTLY, HOWEVER, WITHOUT SUGGESTING THAT A HAS FAILED TO ACT AS A COMPETENT PROFESSIONAL <innMEET-A. J MAKES AN INDIRECT CLARIFICATION REQUEST.

(5) ˙I ˙MĒAN,/
A

A. OVERLAP WITH 4.

PC
BRISK TEMPO.
KC
LITTLE MOVEMENT.
X
THIS IS ACTUALLY A CONTINUATION OF THE PREVIOUS UTTERANCE WITH ITS MESSAGE THAT 'PASS' IS A NEUTRAL TERM. IT MAY ACTUALLY BE AN OFFER TO EXPLICATE THE PRIOR UTTERANCE, IT MAY BE A HEDGE AGAINST POSSIBLE CLAIM OF VIOLATION OF THE CP, IT MAY BE INTENDED AS AN INTRODUCTION TO THE EXPLICATION WHICH DOES FOLLOW,

THAT IS, IT MAY BE THAT J INTERRUPTED WHAT WAS INTENDED AS A CONTINUING UTTERANCE. OR IT MAY REPRESENT FURTHER MANIFESTATION OF TENSION AND UNCERTAINTY.

THIS AMBIGUITY ABOUT THE STATUS OF THIS UTTERANCE, WHICH CAN BE INTERPRETED AS EITHER AN ATTEMPT TO HOLD THE FLOOR OR AS AN INVITATION TO BE INVITED TO EXPLICATE PRIOR UTTERANCE OR SIMPLY AS TENSION AND UNCERTAINTY, IS UNDERLINED IN ITS REPETITION, WHICH FOLLOWS.

I

INTERACTIONAL SIGNIFICANCE IS UNCLEAR.

PC

THE TWO PREVIOUS, OVERLAPPING, UTTERANCES (I.E. 4 AND 5) BEGIN AND END SIMULTANEOUSLY. THIS UTTERANCE (I.E. 6) BEGINS SIMULTANEOUSLY WITH (7), BUT APPEARS TO BE OF LOWER AMPLITUDE THAN (5).

KC

BETWEEN (5) AND (6) A OPENS MOUTH BUT DOES NOT SPEAK. IN THE COURSE OF THIS BRIEF UTTERANCE A SHIFTS ORIENTATION TO S. UTTERANCE IS PUNCTUATED BY SLIGHT GESTICULATION WITH R HAND.

X

SEE (5).

I

UNCLEAR.

PC

INITIAL PART OF UTTERANCE IS HESITANT, UNEVEN, AND CONTAINS A SELF-INTERRUPTION AND CORRECTION. THIS MAY BE A MANIFESTATION OF TENSION. THE LATTER PART

(6)
A. /*(I $\left\{ {KNOW \atop MEAN} \right\}$ IS)/

A. OVERLAP WITH 7.

(7)
S. / .I DON'T₊/

WE DON'T NEED, NŎ. AH, ŬH, WHĂT ĂRE YŎU

*LOOKING* FOR. /ALLEN./ B

A. OVERLAP WITH 6.

B. OVERLAP WITH 8.

OF THE UTTERANCE IS SMOOTH, WITH STRESS ON *LOOKING*. THIS SEEMS MORE LIKE WHAT L-F (47) HAVE CALLED 'NEUTRALITY'.

KC

HAS BEEN ORIENTED TO A SINCE BEGINNING OF EPISODE AND CONTINUES TO BE THROUGHOUT PRODUCTION OF THIS UTTERANCE. (STARTED TO LOOK IN DIRECTION OF J DURING (4) BUT DID NOT COMPLETE MOVEMENT.) MODEST GESTICU-LATION OF L HAND.

X

I DON'T UNDERSTAND WHAT YOU'RE ATTEMPTING TO DO ALLEN, OR WHAT YOU'RE ATTEMPTING TO ELICIT FROM J. WE DON'T NEED ANYTHING MORE FROM J THAN WHAT HE HAS ALREADY PROVIDED IN HIS STATEMENT THAT THE CANDIDATE'S PERFORMANCE WARRANTS A 'PASS'. BUT, I'M NOT SURE THAT THAT IS WHAT YOU'RE ATTEMPTING TO DO BY WHAT YOU ARE SAYING. WHAT INFORMATION ARE YOU TRYING TO ELICIT – WHAT DO YOU WANT J TO SAY? YOU ARE ENGAGED IN SOME SORT OF ATTEMPT AT MANIPULATION – THE GOAL YOU SEEK IS UNCLEAR.

DIRECT ADDRESS MAY MEAN 'REMEMBER WHO YOU ARE AND BEHAVE PROFESSIONALLY'. SUCH AN INTERPRETATION WOULD BE CONGRUENT WITH THE ALT. X AND I FOR (1) AND (3).

I

S AGREES THAT A $<nGP\text{-}M\text{-}A$ HAS VIOLATED THE MAXIM OF MANNER AND REQUESTS THAT A CLARIFY MEANING. HE APPEARS FURTHER TO DENY APPROPRIATENESS OF A'S INVOCATION OF EVALUATION OBLIGATION $<?APPROPRIATE\text{-}MOE$ AND POSSIBLY EVEN TO QUESTION THE VALIDITY OF THE PROPOSITION ITSELF $<?n?\text{-}MOE>$. HE ALSO IMPLIES

POSSIBLE VIOLATION, BY A, OF COLLEGIAL CRITICISM PROPOSITION <*nCRIT*. THROUGH THESE MOVES HE IMPLICITLY CHALLENGES <?*COMP-A*> A'S COMPETENCE. CHALLENGE IS MITIGATED THROUGH THE USE OF FIRST-NAME DIRECT ADDRESS.

PC

*WELL*, IS USED AS A TEMPORISING AND DELAYING FEATURE AND IS FOLLOWED BY SPEECH WHICH IS MARKED BY VERY CONSIDERABLE REPETITION AND APPARENT RELUCTANCE TO COME TO POINT. 'GUESS' AND MODIFER 'SOME' APPEAR TO BE USED AS QUALIFYING DISCLAIMERS. THE LAST PART OF THE UTTERANCE IS ALSO MARKED BY REPETITION – BUT IS MORE FLUENT (SMOOTH?) THAN THE BEGINNING.

KC

HAS BEEN ORIENTED TO S THROUGH (7), MOVING FORWARD TO A 'FLIGHT' POSITION WITH A 'QUIZZICAL POSE'. SLIGHT SETTLING AS UTTERANCE ENDS. A IN THIS PERIOD SHOWS VERY CONSIDERABLE MOVEMENT SLIDING BACK IN CHAIR WHILE KEEPING UPPER BODY FORWARD, SHIFTING WEIGHT FROM ONE CHEEK (BUTTOCK) TO ANOTHER, EVEN LIFTING BODY FROM CHAIR WITH ARMS. CONSIDERABLE HAND AND ARM MOVEMENT. SEEMS LIKE SOMETHING THAT SCHEFLEN MIGHT CHARACTERISE AS 'AGGRESSIVE DEFENDING' OR EVEN AS CHALLENGING.

X

SOMETHING SEEMS TO HAVE GONE AWRY IN OUR JOINT INTERACTION. J EITHER CAN'T (BECAUSE HE DOESN'T UNDERSTAND THE RULES) OR WON'T (WILFULLY) UNDERSTAND WHAT I AM IMPLICITLY ASKING HIM TO DO. AND S, WHO USUALLY UNDERSTANDS ME WHEN I TALK INDIRECTLY AND IMPLICITLY INVOKE RULES APPEARS TO BE REACTING LIKE J, BUT TO BE MORE DIRECTLY CHALLENGING ME. I DISCLAIM

(8)

A

A. /*WELL*,/ I'M I'M, I, I, I, JUST –

I *GUESS* I HAVE IN THE BACK OF MY MIND,

THÁT THÁT I WANT TO *BE*, ABLE TO *CONVEY, SOME*

B

SENSE, /OF, OF HOW:, THE COMMITTEE'S

RESPONSE./

A. OVERLAP WITH 7.

B. OVERLAP WITH 9.

[THIS IS, WITH 9, A JOINT CONSTRUCTION.]

ANY RIGHT TO *DEMAND* A RELATIVE EVALUATION (EVEN THOUGH I THINK THE CANDIDATE HAS A RIGHT TO ONE) BUT I WOULD LIKE TO SUGGEST THAT IT WOULD BE NICE IF I COULD REPORT A COLLECTIVE ASSESSMENT TO THE CANDIDATE. I BELIEVE I HAVE BEHAVED PROPERLY BUT I DON'T WANT TO PUT L AT RISK.

I

A RESISTS S'S CLARIFICATION REQUEST. THIS RESISTANCE AND A FURTHER ATTEMPT TO ELICIT A RELATIVE EVALUATION FROM J ARE BOTH MITIGATED BY: (1) EXPRESSION OF TENSION AND LACK OF CONFIDENCE INTERPRETABLE AS ADMISSION OF QUESTIONABLE COMPETENCE <?COMP-A AND; (2) EMPLOYMENT OF A MORE DIRECT (BUT STILL NOT EXPLICIT) AND POSSIBLY RITUAL (CLICHÉD) PROBE. BY DOING THIS A SIMULTANEOUSLY REITERATES CANDIDATES' RIGHTS TO RELATIVE EVALUATIONS <CRE> AND MEMBERS' OBLIGATIONS <MOE> TO PROVIDE THEM *AND* DENIES ANY INTENTION OF CRITICISING <nCRITJ.

PC

MATTER OF FACT, UNHESITANT. LAST WORD PARTLY 'SWALLOWED'.

KC

HEAD NODS AFFIRMATIVELY JUST BEFORE S BEGINS TO SPEAK, UTTERANCE IS ACCOMPANIED BY MODEST PUNCTUATION WITH L HAND, R HAND RAISES AND FOREFINGER TOUCHES EAR. AS THE UTTERANCE ENDS S AGAIN NODS AFFIRMATIVELY (SOMEWHAT MORE VIGOROUSLY) AND POINTS TOWARD J – WITHOUT LOOKING AT J.

X

NOW I SEE WHAT YOU ARE SAYING. YOU ARE SAYING THAT YOU WANT TO BE ABLE TO TELL THE CANDIDATE HOW WE GRADE HER ON HER DISSERTATION AND ON HER PERFORM-

(9) ·̇/ŎH. THE COMMITTEE'S *RESPONSE* ᴬ

TO THE ENTERPRISE AS A WHOLE./

A. OVERLAP WITH 8.

ANCE TODAY. (THE 'AS A WHOLE' *MAY* ALSO IMPLY SOME KIND OF ASSESSMENT OF FUTURE PROSPECTS – THIS IS NOT CLEAR.) I SEE ALSO THAT YOU HAVE BEEN TRYING TO BE TACTFUL (?) IN YOUR ATTEMPT TO ELICIT J'S CONTRIBUTION TO A COLLECTIVE ASSESSMENT, I WILL JOIN YOU IN STATING THE REQUEST IN A RITUAL MANNER.

(SIMULTANEOUS MESSAGE TO J.) LET'S DECIDE ON A JOINT EVALUATION FOR A TO REPORT TO J. THERE WAS A LESS OBSCURE WAY FOR HIM TO FORMULATE HIS REQUEST TO YOU – AND I HAVE HELPED HIM TO DO THAT.

I

S ACCEPTS A'S OFFERING OF DISAMBIGUATION AND CLARI-FICATION AND, INDEED, ACTUALLY PARTICIPATES IN THE JOINT PRODUCTION OF A (STILL SOMEWHAT INDIRECT) REQUEST FOR A RELATIVE EVALUATION, THEREBY VALI-DATING THE PROPOSITION THAT COMMITTEE MEMBERS HAVE AN OBLIGATION TO PROVIDE SUCH EVALUATIONS <*MOE* AND THAT J HAS NOT DONE SO BUT, THROUGH USE OF INDIREC-TION, AVOIDS QUESTIONING J'S COMPETENCE <*CRIT*>. BY IMPLICATION HE JOINS IN A'S REQUEST THAT J PROVIDE A RELATIVE EVALUATION.

*NOTE*: THE FACT THAT S JOINS WITH A IN JUSTIFICATION OF THE REQUEST FOR A RELATIVE EVALUATION WOULD APPEAR TO WEAKEN THE ALTERNATIVE INTERACTIONAL ANALYSES PROVIDED FOR UTTERANCES (1) AND (3).

COMMENT

IT APPEARS THAT THE JOINT PRODUCTION OF A AND S MAY REPRESENT A SPECIAL CASE OF EMPLOYMENT OF FORMULAIC SPEECH IN INTERACTION, IN THIS INSTANCE AS A KIND OF INDIRECT EUPHEMISM FOR A REQUEST. THE CASE IS SPECIAL IN SEVERAL PARTICULARS. FIRST, IT IS NOT CLEAR FOR WHAT POPULATION THE EXPRESSION, 'CONVEY SOME SENSE

OF X TO Y', IS FORMULAIC. IT IS APPARENTLY SHARED BY A AND S; P'S CONFIRMING GRUNT (10) AND J'S SUBSEQUENT EXPANSION OF HIS EVALUATION SEEMS TO INDICATE THAT THE LATTER TWO ALSO SHARE IT. IT MAY BE LOCAL, IT MAY BE 'ACADEMIC TALK', IT MAY BE 'COMMITTEE TALK'. (THE USE OF 'ENTERPRISE' IS IN THIS CONTEXT, AND IN THIS UTTERANCE, ALSO FORMULAIC – AT LEAST FOR MANY SOCIOLOGISTS.)

THE CASE IS ALSO SPECIAL IN THAT WHILE THE EXPRESSION IS SUCCESSFUL IN GENERATING THE KIND OF DETAILED RESPONSE WHICH WAS APPARENTLY BEING SOUGHT, THE 'REQUEST' REMAINED *VERY* INDIRECT. THE EXPRESSION INCLUDES NO REFERENCE TO THE NOTION OF RELATIVE EVALUATION (AND EVEN S'S 'ENTERPRISE AS A WHOLE' SEEMS TO BE SWALLOWED) AND NO EXPLICIT REFERENCE TO *J'S* OBLIGATION. THE BURDEN OF INTERPRETATION LIES HEAVILY ON THE RECIPIENT – J'S SUCCESS IN MAKING THE INTENDED INTERPRETATION MAKES PLAUSIBLE AN INFERENCE WHICH SAYS THAT SHARED UNDERSTANDINGS ARE BEING FORMULAICALLY INVOKED.

PC

VERY SOFT AND QUIET – COMES IMMEDIATELY AFTER (8) AND (9) ARE SIMULTANEOUSLY COMPLETED.

KC

BEGINS HEAD MOVEMENT TO LEFT (IN DIRECTION OF J) AT SAME TIME UTTERANCE IS MADE. THIS IS AS MUCH DISENGAGEMENT FROM A AS GAZE TOWARD J – WHICH IS NOT INITIATED UNTIL J ACTUALLY BEGINS TO SPEAK. IT IS RATHER THE BEGINNING OF A 'CONFIRMATORY NOD' WHICH BEGINS WITH UTTERANCE AND ENDS IMMEDIATELY AFTER J BEGINS TALKING.

X

SO THAT'S WHAT THAT WAS ALL ABOUT. I SEE NOW WHAT A WAS DRIVING AT. HOW ARE YOU GOING TO RESPOND, J?

I

NO JUDGEMENT OF P'S PERCEPTION OF THE LEGITIMACY OF THE REQUEST CAN BE INFERRED FROM HER (P'S) BEHAVIOUR. SHE IS SIMPLY NOTING HER COMPREHENSION OF THE PRIOR EXCHANGE AND EXPRESSING INTEREST (BY SHIFT IN ORIENTATION) IN J'S RESPONSE. THE FORMULAIC EXPRESSION OF COMPREHENSION WOULD SEEM TO IMPLY, HOWEVER, THAT SHE ALSO AGREED WITH J'S ASSERTION THAT A HAD VIOLATED THE GENERAL PRINCIPLE OF CP, THAT IS, $< nCP\text{-}M\text{-}A$.

# Notes

*This paper was originally prepared for presentation at the International Conference on Social Psychology and Language sponsored by the Social Psychology section of the British Psychological Society and held at the University of Bristol in July, 1979. I am grateful to Professors W. Peter Robinson and Paul Werth for inviting me to revise the paper for inclusion in this volume, and to many others for critical readings and suggestions. Partial funding for the MAP has been provided by the National Science Foundation, the Grant Foundation, and the Social Science Research Council (USA) and is gratefully acknowledged. I am also thankful to Indiana University for its support of the project.

1. Strawson (1964), in his critical exegesis and extension of Grice (1957), suggests that S has four ends in mind in directing an utterance to H (the first three are Grice's, the fourth Strawson's addition):

   (i) that H do (believe) r;
   (ii) that H recognize that utterance is intended to produce r;
   (iii) that H do (or believe) r, at least in part, because of utterance;
   (iv) that H recognize that utterance is intended to inform H and S wants r
        (i.e. that H recognise utterance as INSTRUMENTALITY).

Strawson remarks that additional conditions (specified ends) may be required in order to characterise an utterance as representing an instance of attempted communication, but concludes that whether or not those listed are sufficient they are certainly necessary.

In the cases of some INSTRUMENTALITIES, e.g. *bamboozle, cajole, con*, etc., of course, S's (ii) and (iv) intentions may not hold.

2. For some highly suggestive exceptions to this general neglect see e.g. Melbin (1972), Scheflen (1973), Cole and Morgan (1975), Labov and Fanshel (1977), Brown and Levinson (1978), Atkinson and Drew (1979) and Heise (1979). No one can work in this area without attending to the work of Goffman. One can, of course, go back (as Goffman has) to Burke (e.g. 1968; see also Overington 1977).

3. The principal aim of ethnomethodology and related projects has been the examination of just such 'taken-for-granteds'. For useful introductions to the epistemological arguments undergirding the enthnomethdological and related (i.e. conversational analysis) perspectives see, illustratively, Garfinkel (1967), Cicourel (1974), Mehan and Wood (1975) and Atkinson and Drew (1979).

4. There is a substantial literature on indirect speech acts. See, for a sampling, Searle (1975), Bates (1976), Ervin-Tripp (1976), Labov and Fanshel (1977) and Brown and Levinson (1978).

5. It is the *behaviour* labelled by certain verbs (or, sometimes, by descriptions incorporating verbs), and *not the verbs themselves*, which is the focus of my investigation and which I am calling INSTRUMENTALITIES.

6. For a distinction between **mishearings** and **misunderstandings** (the latter a deliberate *act*) see 6.1, *infra.*, and, for a somewhat more complete treatment, Grimshaw (1980b).

7. Grimshaw (1980a) addresses issues of social appropriateness (with regard to both selection and reporting of INSTRUMENTALITIES) somewhat more comprehensively.

8. Sources of support for the MAP are listed in the acknowledgements. A history of the project and its genesis, descriptions of the data and of the data record, and brief descriptions of tentatively projected analyses by the several participants are available on request.

9. Two other events were filmed and recorded: (i) a student faculty committee meeting about a graduate programme and (ii) a graduate student meeting ostensibly

on the same topic. The first was unsatisfactory on theoretical grounds (it was largely a monologue by the committee chair – a faculty member); the second could not be used because one participant refused to sign a release (ethical considerations would have excluded its use, at least for some years, in any event). The data records have been archived.

10. It is a truism that all social interaction has some significance to the social actors involved; it is also true that some events are perceived by participants as being more important than others. MAP analysts, members of sponsoring bodies and project consultants generally agreed that events in which consequential decisions are made are ordinarily more important to participants than are 'casual conversations'. (The quotation marks are used to acknowledge that casual conversations may be anything but casual for participants who are, for example, intent on 'impression management' or subject to intimidation.) Events which have salience for participants include, among others, (i) those in which interactants of sharply different power negotiate mutual expectations, (ii) critical junctures in careers, (iii) meetings to allocate scarce and desired resources, (iv) discussions directed at selection of goals and strategies in social undertakings. Each of the interactions recorded included such events.

11. The bulk of the studies which have intensively analysed speech events has been of dyadic interaction (the therapy groups analysed by Scheflen and by Sacks and his associates constitute important exceptions). Small groups researchers have concluded that 'the pair and the three-person group have special characteristics of intimacy and power which give each group some unique aspects' and that 'although the optimum size for a group varies with the task of the group, a five-man group is found to have some advantages for problems which can be solved by group discussion' (Hare 1962:225). There are other size-related considerations. For example, it has been observed (though not considered in detail) that, topics and other factors held constant, the likelihood of sub-conversations fragmenting off increases rapidly as groups get larger. Additionally, within any given period of interaction increased numbers of participants proportionally reduce the extent of average verbal participation. Finally, continuous full-body filming and audio recording of participants become more difficult as larger numbers of actors are involved. For these reasons, each of the events filmed had five members, a number which permitted avoidance both of the particularities of smaller groups and the fragmentation potential and technical recording difficulties of larger ones.

12. The film paradigm employed in MAP data collection was that of Researchable Film Observation (Feld and Williams 1975, n.d.). For a discussion of collection of sound-image data for research on social interaction see Grimshaw (1978, forthcoming).

13. There is a detailed record of the MAP itself which will be used, at a later date, as the basis for an ethnography of the MAP as a collaborative project.

14. The Labov and Fanshel explication of their procedures is clear and comprehensive. For a shorter summary see Grimshaw (1979).

15. I have used topic shifts as boundaries of episodes.

16. The appendix incorporates alternative expansions and characterisations of interaction offered by one of my MAP colleagues.

17. Labov and Fanshel are thoroughly circumspect in their discussion of imputations of intent, noting both its ambiguous status and the fact that their evidence is abstract and indirect (see especially p. 346). Their perspective is, such reservations notwithstanding, quintessentially sociological, as when they observe, 'In any over-all view, it is obvious that actions are more important than utterances, since it is actions that have consequences and affect other people's lives', and that, 'The action is what is *intended* in that it expresses how the speaker means to affect the listener, to move him, to cause him to respond' (p. 59).

Questions of intent are sticky. While I believe they are generally best left to the philosophers who so enjoy them, I have looked at them briefly in my attempt to distinguish mishearing and misunderstanding (1980b).

18. A somewhat more detailed, but also more *ad hoc*, interpretation of the text used here appears in Grimshaw (1980a).

19. An additional distinction must be made between linguistic and pragmatic (functional or social semantic) 'misunderstandings'. Examples of the former might include assignment of different (i.e. other than those intended by S) lexical meanings to words with multiple dictionary entries (or, if the context is felicitous, meanings of homonyms) or of reinterpretation of phonological production. Examples of the latter would include responding to indirect requests as if they were, indeed, interrogatives or statements. It is not clear whether this is a genuine dichotomy or whether, like grammaticality, it constitutes a linear continuum.

20. Such reactions by S can, of course, be very complex acts reflecting S's rationalisation in the face of power or other attributes of H (or an audience) which would make a confrontation too costly. The presence and characteristics of an audience may in themselves constrain S's reactions (as they also do H's behaviours).

# References

Albert, E.M. (1972) 'Culture patterning of speech behavior in Burundi' in J. Gumperz and D. Hymes (eds.), *Directions in Sociolinguistics*, Holt, Rinehart and Winston, New York, pp. 72–105

Atkinson, J.M. and P. Drew (1979) *Order in Court*, Humanities Press, Atlantic Highlands, New Jersey

Bates, E. (1976) *Language and Context: the Acquisition of Pragmatics*, Academic Press, New York

Brown, R. and A. Gilman (1960), 'The Pronouns of power and solidarity' in T. Sebeok (ed.), *Style in Language*, Wiley, New York, pp. 253–76

Brown, P. and S. Levinson (1978) 'Universals in language usage: politeness phenomena' in E.N. Goody (ed.), *Questions and Politeness: Strategies in Social Interaction*, Cambridge University Press, Cambridge, pp. 59–289

Burke, K. (1968) 'Dramatism' in D. Sills (ed.), *International Encyclopedia of the Social Sciences*, Macmillan and The Free Press, New York, pp. 445–52

Cicourel, A.V. (1974) *Cognitive Sociology: Language and Meaning in Social Interaction*, The Free Press, New York

Cole, P. and J.L. Morgan (eds.) (1975) *Syntax and Semantics, 3: Speech Acts*, Academic Press, New York

Cook-Gumperz, J. and W. Corsaro (1977) 'Social-ecological constraints on children's communicative strategies', *Sociology, 11, 3*, pp. 411–34

Corsaro, W. (1979) 'We're friends, right? children's use of access rituals in a nursery school', *Language in Society*, 8, 3, pp. 315–36

Ervin-Tripp, S. (1976) 'Is Sybil there? The structure of some American English directives', *Language in Society, 5, 1*, pp. 25–66

Feld, S. and C. Williams (1975) 'Toward a researchable film language', *Studies in the Anthropology of Visual Communication, 2, 1*, pp. 25–32

–– (n.d.) 'Generating Researchable Film Observations', *Working Papers in Culture and Communication, 1, 2*, pp. 62–75

Garfinkel, H. (1967) *Studies in Ethnomethodology*, Prentice-Hall, Englewood Cliffs, New Jersey

Goffman, E. (1971) *Relations in Public: Microstudies of the Public Order*, Basic Books, New York

—— (1974) *Frame Analysis: An Essay on the Organization of Experience*, Harper and Row, New York

Goody, E. (ed.) (1978) *Questions and Politeness: Strategies in Social Interaction*, Cambridge University Press, Cambridge

Gordon, D. and G. Lakoff (1975) 'Conversational postulates', in P. Cole and J.L. Morgan (eds.) *Syntax and Semantics, 3: Speech Acts*, Academic Press, New York, pp. 83–106

Grice, H.P. (1957) 'Meaning', *The Philosophical Review, 66, 3*, pp. 377–88

—— (1975) 'Logic and conversation' in P. Cole and J.L. Morgan (eds.) *Syntax and Semantics, 3: Speech Acts*, Academic Press, New York, pp. 43–58

Grimshaw, A.D. (1978) 'The collection of sound-image data for research on social interaction', mimeo paper, Indiana University

—— (1979) 'What's Been Done – When All's Been Said', *Contemporary Sociology, 8, 2*, pp. 170–6

—— (1980a) 'Selection and labeling of INSTRUMENTALITIES of verbal manipulation', *Discourse Processes, 3, 3*, pp. 203–29

—— (1980b) 'Let's hear it for H: mishearings, misunderstandings and other non-successes in talk', *Sociological Inquiry, 50, 3-4*

—— (forthcoming) 'The "other" kind of data tapes: visual and audio recording of social interaction', *Sociological Methods and Research*

Grimshaw, A.D. and L. Holden (1976) 'Postchildhood modifications of linguistic and social competence', *Items, 30, 3*, pp. 33–42

Halliday, M.A.K. and R. Hasan (1976) *Cohesion in English*, Longman Group, London

Hare, A.P. (1962) *Handbook of Small Group Research*, The Free Press, New York

Heider, F. (1958) *The Psychology of Interpersonal Relations*, Wiley, New York

Heise, D. (1979) *Understanding Events*, Cambridge University Press, Cambridge

Hymes, D. (1974) *Foundations in Sociolinguistics: An Ethnographic Approach*, University of Pennsylvania Press, Philadelphia

Labov, W. and D. Fanshel (1977) *Therapeutic Discourse: Psychotherapy as Conversation*, Academic Press, New York

Mehan, H. and H. Wood (1975) *The Reality of Ethnomethodology*, Wiley, New York

Melbin, M. (1972) *Alone and with Others: A Grammar of Interpersonal Behavior*, Harper and Row, New York

Mitchell-Kernan, C. and S. Ervin-Tripp (eds.) (1977) *Child Discourse*, Academic Press, New York

Overington, M. (1977) 'Kenneth Burke and the method of Dramatism', *Theory and Society, 4*, pp. 131–56

Sacks, H., E. Schegloff and G. Jefferson (1974) 'A Simplest Systematics for the Organisation of Turntaking for Conversation', *Language, 50, 4*, 696–735

Searle, J. (1969) *Speech Acts: An Essay in the Philosophy of Language*, Cambridge University Press, Cambridge

—— (1975) 'Indirect speech acts', in P. Cole and J.L. Morgan (eds.) *Syntax and Semantics, 3: Speech Acts*, Academic Press, New York, pp. 59–82

Scheflen, A.E. (1973) *Communicational Structure: Analysis of a Psychotherapy Transaction*, Indiana University Press, Bloomington, Indiana

Sinclair, J. McH. and R.M. Coulthard (1975) *Towards an Analysis of Discourse: The English Used by Teachers and Pupils*, Oxford University Press, London

Strawson, P.F. (1964) 'Intention and convention in speech acts', *The Philosophical Review, 73, 4*, pp. 439–60

# 3 SOME STRATEGIES FOR SUSTAINING CONVERSATION

## Gordon Wells, Margaret MacLure and Martin Montgomery

Despite the pervasive conviction, shared alike by participants in conversations and analysts of those conversations, that there is pattern and order in the succession of contributions of which they are constituted, the organisational principles which underlie this orderliness have proved remarkably resistant to formal description.[1] Two features of conversation which contribute to the analyst's problems are, first, the manner in which the orderliness unfolds moment by moment in the local here-and-now of the interaction and, secondly, the fact that there is no one-to-one correspondence between the forms of utterances and the conversational functions that they perform in particular contexts. Is it possible, therefore, to make generalised statements about structure that will have some predictive value, yet at the same time give due recognition to the complex, on-the-spot creativity that conversationalists display in particular contexts? Can a description be given of the 'abstract resources' that Schenkein refers to, when he describes conversation as 'organised through abstract resources bearing on locally idiosyncratic conversational environments' (1978:3)?

Our own interest in these problems stems from our attempt to trace the development of conversational skills in children and to investigate the contributions that different styles of conversation make to children's learning. The data we are working with consist of recordings of spontaneous talk between young children and their parents and teachers, and it is on the basis of analysis of this material that we are constructing a descriptive framework that we hope will also apply to other types of discourse.[2] Since a fairly full exposition of this framework has been presented elsewhere (Wells, Montgomery and MacLure 1979) we shall restrict ourselves on this occasion to the discussion of an elaboration of one aspect of the model.

## The Sequential Organisation of Discourse

Perhaps the most salient feature of discourse, and the one that attests

73

most strongly to the existence of orderliness, is the prevalence of pairs of utterances that are both structurally and functionally linked, e.g. question-answer, request-comply, inform-acknowledge. However, analysis of discourse solely in terms of such 'adjacency pairs' as they have been called (Schegloff and Sacks 1973) is not entirely satisfactory for two reasons. First, they do not account for all the structurally related sequences of utterances that can be recognised in texts, and so cannot provide a firm basis for a descriptive framework that will account for complete texts; secondly, the form in which the description is made fails to distinguish between the indefinitely extendable list of speech acts that speakers may perform and the strictly limited types of structural organisation through which these acts are realised.

Following other linguists, therefore, (e.g. Sinclair and Coulthard 1975; Halliday 1977) we prefer to start with a more abstract category, the **exchange**. This we define as consisting of two structural positions: an **initiating** move by a first speaker and a **responding** move by a second speaker. The exchange is thus the minimal unit from which longer stretches of discourse are constructed. On the paradigmatic axis, the move types which can fill the two syntagmatically-defined positions are derived from the basic dynamics of any social interchange — whether verbal or non-verbal (cf. Halliday 1977). That is, in opening any social exchange, a participant can either GIVE something to the other participant or SOLICIT something from him. The respondent then completes the exchange by, respectively, ACKNOWLEDGING what has been given or GIVING what has been solicited. Within the one syntagmatic structure there are thus two basic types of exchange:

   (i) **Initiate**: SOLICIT  — **Respond**: GIVE.
   (ii) **Initiate**: GIVE  — **Respond**: ACKNOWLEDGE.

On to one or other of these basic exchange types can be mapped the whole range of reciprocally related speech-acts, including those identified as adjacency pairs:

     *SOLICIT – GIVE*          *GIVE – ACKNOWLEDGE*
     REQUEST – COMPLY      ASSERTION – AGREEMENT.
     QUESTION – ANSWER      STATEMENT OF INTENTION –
                                EVALUATION.
     INVITATION –           COMPLIMENT – ACCEPTANCE.
       ACCEPTANCE, etc.

Thus far we have described a basic structure of discourse, the single exchange, and shown how it is related to more functionally-oriented descriptions of discourse organisation. However, most conversations consist of longer stretches of related exchanges, even where small children are involved as participants (cf. Keenan 1977). One way in which such longer stretches may be built up is simply by chaining a series of topically-related exchanges one after another.

In this pattern, typified by a teacher asking questions around a class, following each response by a further question on the same, or a related, topic, the coherence that is perceived stems partly from the repeated exchange structure of question and answer, and partly from semantic continuity realised through syntactic and lexical cohesive links between the separate exchanges. The following is an example of such a conversation involving a rather younger child:

1. Father: Where did Pappy go yesterday? Seaside?
   Mark:    Seaside.
   Father: Who did he go with?
   Mark:    With Pappy ə Nanna ə Pappy.
   Father: And Paul?
   Mark:    An Paul.
   Father: And Sandra?
   Mark:    An Sandra.

                                                    (Mark, 26½ months)

However, conversations built on this pattern alone are not very common. Much more frequent, with parents and teachers alike, is the use of strategies that extend the first exchange by linking a further exchange to it, thereby sustaining the child's participation. The resulting structures we term **sequences**. One very common linking device is to produce an utterance which, while responding to a prior initiation, simultaneously initiates a further exchange. For convenience, we shall refer to utterances which combine the responding position in one exchange with the initiating position in another as occurring in a CONTINUING position in the sequence.[3] Continues are found at various points in the unfolding of a sequence and draw upon a variety of syntactic and intonational options for their realisation. One obvious syntactic mechanism is the addition of a tag:

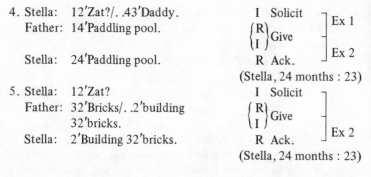

```
2. Stella:   Zat?                          I   Solicit   ⌐ Ex 1
   Father:   That's a carpet-sweeper isn't  {R}
             it like Mummy's?               {I} Give     ⌐
   Stella:   Yes like Mummy's.             R   Ack.      ⌐ Ex 2
                                       (Stella, 24 months : 23)
3. Mark:     Where's Pappa's pen draw on    I   Solicit  ⌐ Ex 1
             there?                         {R}
   Mother:   You left it at Clifton didn't  {I} Give      ⌐
             you?
   Mark:     No.⁴                          R   Ack.      ⌐ Ex 2
                                          (Mark, 30 months)
```

In both these examples it is the addition of a tag to the parent's move which, in these particular contexts, makes them response-demanding, and thus non-terminal.

A similar effect can be achieved through intonation (cf. Appendix for conventions of transcription):

```
4. Stella:   12'Zat?/. .43'Daddy.          I   Solicit  ⌐ Ex 1
   Father:   14'Paddling pool.             {R}
                                           {I} Give      ⌐
   Stella:   24'Paddling pool.            R   Ack.      ⌐ Ex 2
                                       (Stella, 24 months : 23)
5. Stella:   12'Zat?                        I   Solicit  ⌐
   Father:   32'Bricks/. .2'building       {R}
             32'bricks.                     {I} Give      ⌐
   Stella:   2'Building 32'bricks.         R   Ack.      ⌐ Ex 2
                                       (Stella, 24 months : 23)
```

Although the second of these examples involves rising tone on the utterance heard as a Continue, this is not true of the first, which has a high fall. What is common to the two examples is that they both involve high pitch, and it is this that seems to mark them as setting up expectations of a further response.

As we mentioned above, one of the simplest ways of creating longer stretches of internally organised conversation is by the simple chaining of semantically-related exchanges. However, an alternative to the simple repetition of the Pattern A initiate, B respond, is for B to make two moves within one turn, the first completing one exchange and the second initiating another, e.g.

6. Luke:  Ladybird (pointing to picture). I Give  ] Ex 1
 Adult: Yes.          R Ack.

    It's a big one too.     I Give  ] Ex 2
 Luke: Big one.        R Ack.

              (Luke, 25 months)

Frequently, as in the above example, such chains consist of exchanges of the GIVE-ACKNOWLEDGE type. Where this is the case, a further possibility exists for linking the two exchanges structurally by making the ACKNOWLEDGE in the first exchange only *implicitly*, proceeding straight to the initiation of the next exchange without an overt marking of ACKNOWLEDGMENT. This produces another type of CONTINUE which, in such cases, may take the form of a further GIVE or, as in the following example, of a Solicit:

7. Rosie: And 2′I got a 23′bed.    I GIVE  ] Ex 1
 Teacher: 3′Where's your 34′bed?  {R} (ACK.)
              {I }SOLICIT ] Ex 2
 Rosie: E's 34up′stairs.      R GIVE

 Teacher: Anybody else got a 242′bed
    in your room?
 Rosie: Carol got a 321′bed/and
    342′Kelvin/. and 34′Carol.
 Teacher: ↑14 Um′hum.

       . . . . .

 Rosie: When I gets 143′up/ I creeps  I GIVE  ] Ex 1
    in 34′Mummy's bed.
 Teacher: For 243 a′nother cuddle?  {R} (ACK.)
              {I }SOLICIT ] Ex 2
 Rosie: (nods)        R GIVE

         (Rosie 5½ years. LHS 2)

In all these different examples a CONTINUE occurs when the participant who is cast in the role of respondent in the first exchange produces an utterance which simultaneously initiates a further exchange. It is thus designed by its producer to sustain the discourse and in adult-child talk is most likely to occur when the child is the initiator of the first exchange.

Where it is the adult, on the other hand, who is the initiator of the first exchange, the CONTINUE strategy is not available. However, there is an alternative, which has a similar effect of sustaining the discourse beyond a single exchange. As we saw earlier, GIVE moves can occur in either position in the structure of the exchange: as response to an initiating SOLICIT or as initiation to which an ACKNOWLEDGE is the expected response. In an exchange initiated by a Solicit, the dual potential of the GIVE move which occurs as response can be exploited by the original initiator treating it as a further initiation, to which an ACKNOWLEDGE may be given as a response:

8. Teacher: Who knows what ice is?           I   SOLICIT ⎤ Ex 1
   Pupil:   I have that in my drink at      { R }GIVE    ⎦
            home.                           { (I) }      ⎤
   Teacher: That's right.                    R  ACK.     ⎦ Ex 2

                         (Jacqueline, 5¼ years : CL2R)

Here, following a GIVE in response to an initial SOLICIT, the teacher treats that GIVE as an initiation to which she provides a responding ACKNOWLEDGE. The () round the I in the second exchange indicates that, in providing the GIVE in response to the initial SOLICIT, the respondent need have no intention of initiating a further exchange: rather, it is the first speaker who, exploiting the latent opportunity for GIVES to receive ACKNOWLEDGES, retroactively constitutes the response as the initiation of a second exchange by providing that ACKNOWLEDGEMENT. Here again, the linking move combines response and initiation positions, but the combination in this case is imposed after the event by the original initiator.

Sinclair and Coulthard (1975) describe the structural position of the 'retroactive ACKNOWLEDGE' as a FOLLOW-UP and this is a very apt description. However, where they treat it as the third position in a basic three-part exchange, which they consider to be particularly characteristic of teacher-pupil interaction, we wish to treat it, like the CONTINUE position, as a device for linking two exchanges to form a longer sequence.[5] At the same time it should be pointed out that the FOLLOW-UP strategy is not restricted to contexts like the classroom, where the opening SOLICIT calls for a display of knowledge or competence, and where the final ACKNOWLEDGE is usually some kind of evaluation, as can be seen from example 9. Here it is Thomas who initiates the sequence with a SOLICIT and follows up in the second exchange with an ACKNOWLEDGE.

9. Thomas: What's ə down there?          I   SOLICIT ⎤
   Adult:   That's the tape recorder.   ⎰R⎱GIVE         ⎬ Ex 2
                                        ⎱(I)⎰             
   Thomas: 'corder.                      R  ACK.      ⎦ Ex 2
                                        (Thomas, 27 months)

Secondly, not all teacher questions inexorably lead to a FOLLOW-UP, as can be seen in example 7, where, following Rosie's response in exchange 2, the teacher initiates a new, topically-related exchange.

The final linking strategy that we will discuss may at first sight seem rather different. Following any move in a sequence, the recipient of that move may produce a move which is a SOLICIT rather than the GIVE or ACKNOWLEDGE that is anticipated — but which is nevertheless not heard as inappropriate, e.g.:

10. Mark:   3ə fwa (= can I have water?)   I   SOLICIT  ⎤ Ex 1
    Mother: What?                        ⎰Ret⎱SOLICIT  ⎦
                                         ⎱I  ⎰          ⎤ Ex 2
    Mark:   3 ə fwa                      ⎰R ⎱GIVE       ⎦
                                         ⎱I₂⎰SOLICIT  ⎤ Ex 3
    Mother: No                            R  GIVE      ⎦
                                         (Mark, 23½ months)

Instances such as these have often been analysed as creating some sort of embedded structure, with one exchange intervening between the start and the completion of another (Jefferson 1972). To account, within the framework being developed here, for the fact that we hear such SOLICITS as (i) initiating a further exchange, (ii) somehow taking account of the previous move, and (iii) allowing a subsequent resumption of the matter in that previous move, we introduce the structural category RETURN, which in these cases replaces RESPONSE as the second part of an exchange, introducing a bound exchange (i.e. one which cannot stand alone). In the example above, Mother's SOLICIT is a RETURN in that it both initiates a new exchange and, at the same time, takes account in some sense of the preceding initiation. Mark's reply both responds to the immediately preceding initiation and *in so doing* reinitiates the first exchange. Mother's final response then, strictly speaking, only responds to the initiation in the preceding move, but, since this is a *re*-initiation of the utterance which started the sequence, it can be seen how this is heard as some sort of 'retrieval' of the exchange set up by the original initiation. This account, we believe, partially overcomes the problem raised by the notion of 'embedded' or 'inserted' exchanges, with the implication that the ultimate completion of the first exchange can be predicted from the original initiation, independently of the pattern that the intervening exchange(s) may take.

Sequences such as example 10 have been described as 'contingent queries' (Garvey 1977) or 'clarification request sequences' (Corsaro 1977), and 'clarification' certainly seems to be the function of the exchange initiated by 'What?' in the above example. But our data abound in instances of a rather similar pattern, where the child's initiation is followed by an adult utterance which simply repeats the child's utterance with the addition of some modification that signals the expectation of a further response from the child:

11. Mark:    1'Oh Mark got 34'change.
    Mother:  ↑12'oh you've/2'got some 343'change/32'haven't you?
    Mark:    34'Yeh.

                                                    (Mark, 30 months)

12. Stella:   2'Put it 12 a'way.
    Mother:  ↑Put it 121 a'way?
    Stella:   12'Yeh.

                                            (Stella, 24 months : 03)

13. Rosie:   I don't 243'like that one.
    Teacher: You don't 24'like it?
    Rosie:   (shakes head)
    Teacher: 1'Why 243'not?
    Rosie:   I only 2'likes 342'little ones.

                                          (Rosie, 5½years : LHS2)

As we have pointed out elsewhere (Wells and Montgomery, 1981), repetitions in themselves do not set up expectations for a responding move, for they can often be heard as simply acknowledging a preceding GIVE. However, where they are uttered with high pitch or with an added tag, as in these examples, they are invariably followed by a further response.

In some cases, such as examples 12 and 13 above, the function of the response-demanding repetition seems very similar to the direct SOLICIT in example 10, that of checking reception of the previous utterance before extending the matter further. But this is not always the case, as can be seen from example 11. However, what all the examples 10–13 have in common is that, where a purely responding utterance would be expected as the sequel to the initiating move, the second utterance fails to provide the expected response, but rather, itself, calls for a further response. There is clearly some similarity between these examples of sequences involving a RETURN and some of those considered earlier that were linked by a CONTINUE (e.g. 2-5). The essential difference between the two types is that, whereas a CONTINUE is simultaneously both an initiation and a response which takes up the implications of the preceding initiation, in the case of a RETURN the utterance which initiates the linked exchange does not fully satisfy the implicature of the initiation in the first exchange.

## Linked Exchanges and Degrees of Prospectiveness

In the preceding pages we have considered a number of strategies which are used, amongst other reasons, to sustain conversation, by creating sequences of linked exchanges, and thereby extending the point at which closure occurs. As was suggested at the outset, the functions that these devices can serve in the context of particular interactions are extremely various and hardly to be captured within a formal description. However, in structural terms, there does seem to be a limited number of ways of linking exchanges, of which we have described three. In each case, the link is achieved by making one utterance fill two structural positions simultaneously: response in the first exchange and initiation in the second. What sort of combination is involved — CONTINUE, FOLLOW-UP or RETURN — depends upon whether the link is made prospectively or retrospectively, and on the extent to which the new initiation can also be heard as a well-formed response. However, what all these devices have in common is their effect of extending the first exchange in ways that are clearly structural.

At this point, therefore, it may be helpful to see whether there are any further characteristics that are shared by the various types of link. One such feature is the **prospective** force of the linking utterance in each type. The notion of prospectiveness was suggested by Sinclair (1975), and Coulthard and Brazil (1979) make use of an opposition between the prospective and retrospective roles of initiating and responding utterances in their account of the structure of the exchange. However, what was originally put forward as a dichotomy, we propose to treat as a scale, with moves being rated from most strongly to least strongly prospective. At one end of the scale are SOLICITING moves, which are strongly prospective in their expectation of a response;

at the other end are ACKNOWLEDGES, which are very weakly, if at all, prospective, since they always occur in response position. Around the middle of the scale are GIVE moves, which have the potential of functioning as either initiations or responses.

Associated with these three segments of the scale, though by no means in a simple one-to-one relationship with them, are the options in the mood system: wh- and polar interrogatives being associated with SOLICITS, declaratives with GIVES, and a variety of moodless structures and idioms with ACKNOWLEDGES. In a fuller exposition finer distinctions would need to be made between, for example, the relative prospectiveness of wh- as compared with polar interrogatives, or between full and elliptical declaratives.[6] Qualifications would also need to be made concerning the way in which mood interacts with the semantic content of the utterance and with features of the non-verbal context, in arriving at the precise degree of prospectiveness of particular utterances (cf. Davies 1979). Nevertheless, the above correspondences are correct for what might be called 'canonical' cases.

Also associated with the scale of prospectiveness are the intonational options of tone and pitch height: rising tones and high pitch being heard as more strongly prospective with respect to a particular utterance than falling tones or low pitch. These options, together with the syntactic options of adding a tag to a declarative utterance or a 'recipient address term', such as 'Mummy', provide means for increasing the prospectiveness of moves that are not initially strongly prospective in terms of their mood choice. The result is that, as a speaker constructs his move in the context of the ongoing exchange, he or she has available a range of options of varying degrees of prospectiveness, which allows him to influence whether the conversation stops at that point or continues for at least one move beyond the response position in any exchange.

Looked at in terms of the scale of prospectiveness, it can thus be seen that all the linking strategies share the feature of exploiting the possibility of increasing, by syntactic or intonational means, the prospectiveness of moves which follow an initiation. In the sequences involving Continues, moves which, in context, would otherwise be simply GIVES or ACKNOWLEDGES are given increased prospectiveness by the addition of a tag or the choice of high pitch, or by realising the ACKNOWLEDGE only implicitly, thus causing them to function as initiations of further exchanges. Sequences involving FOLLOW-UPS exploit the mid-range of prospectiveness associated with GIVE moves by completing a linked exchange with a move that is weaker in prospectiveness than the preceding GIVE. In sequences involving RETURNS, the initiating move in the bound exchange is upgraded in prospectiveness beyond the level contextually anticipated to such an extent that such moves do not even qualify as self-sufficient responses and are heard as in some sense interrupting the flow of the discourse.

It seems, therefore, that the way in which the various pragmatic functions of utterances investigated by those working in the Austinian tradition of speech acts are mapped onto the sequential organisation of discourse can be partly explained in terms of the way in which the three basic types of move are built into exchanges and sequences through exploitation of the scale of prospectiveness. At this stage, this proposal is no more than a working hypothesis in need of evaluation through the analysis of additional data. If it survives this test, however, it may provide a means of explaining how some of the systems of linguistic form are drawn upon, in context, to achieve the various structural patterns that we recognise in coherent sequences of conversation.

## Notes

1. An earlier version of this paper was presented at the Sixth LACUS Forum, Calgary, August, 1979 and is published in the Proceedings of the Conference.
2. The research programme, 'Language at Home and at School', is supported by grants from the Social Science Research Council. An overview of the research can be found in Wells (1979).
3. Previously (Wells *et al*. 1979) we treated CONTINUE as a third structural position in an extended exchange. We now consider it preferable to treat such cases as sequences of overlapping (linked) exchanges rather than as an alternative structural organisation of the basic exchange.
4. At first sight the classification of this negative response as ACKNOWLEDGE may seem inappropriate. The previous move, GIVE and tag with falling tone, anticipates a confirmatory acknowledgement. However, rejection is always a possible alternative to acceptance in such contexts, even though much less common. The problem is that a negative response seems to introduce a new element into the sequence in a way that is not true of a positive response. An adult would typically follow the negative ACKNOWLEDGE by initiating a new exchange with a GIVE move that explained or justified the rejection. Perhaps the child's next utterance, 'I want it', can, if allowances are made for its egocentricity, be heard in such a way.
5. A fuller formal justification for this decision can be found in Wells *et al*. (1979).
6. In this context, we are aware of having ignored the imperative mood. This decision was taken in the interests of simplicity of exposition, since it requires a rather different form of treatment (cf. Coulthard & Brazil 1979).

## References

Corsaro, W.A. (1977) 'Clarification requests as a feature of adult-child discourse', *Language in Society, 6*, 183–207

Coulthard, R.M. and D. Brazil (1979) *Exchange Structure*, Discourse Analysis Monographs 5, University of Birmingham English Language Research

Davies, E.C. (1979) *On the Semantics of Syntax*, Croom Helm, London

Garvey, C. (1977) The contingent query: a dependent act in conversation, in M. Lewis and L.A. Rosenblum (eds.) *Interaction, Conversation and the Development of Language*, New York

Halliday, M.A.K. (1977) 'Language as code and language as behaviour: a systemic-functional interpretation of the nature and ontogenesis of dialogue', to appear in S.M. Lamb and A. Makkai (eds.) *Semiotics of Culture and Language*

Jefferson, G. (1972) 'Side sequences', in D. Sudnow (ed.) *Studies in Social Interaction*, Free Press, New York

Keenan, E.O. (1977) 'Making it last: repetition in children's discourse', in S.M. Ervin-Tripp & C. Mitchell-Kernan (eds.) *Child Discourse*, Academic Press, New York

Schegloff, E.A. and H. Sacks (1973) 'Opening up closings', *Semiotica, 8, 4*, 289–327

Schenkein, J. (ed.) (1978) *Studies in the Organisation of Conversational Interaction*, Academic Press, New York

Sinclair, J.McH. (1975) *Discourse in relation to language structure and semiotics*, paper presented to Burg Wartenstein Symposium 66: Semiotics of Culture and Language, Vienna, August, 1975 (mimeo)

—— and R.M. Coulthard (1975) *Towards an Analysis of Discourse: the English used by Teachers and Pupils*, Oxford University Press, London

Wells, C.G. (1979) 'Describing children's linguistic development at home and at school', *British Educational Research Journal, 5*, 75–98

—— M.M. Montgomery and M. MacLure (1979), 'Adult-child discourse: outline of a model of analysis', *Journal of Pragmatics, 3*, 337–80

—— and M.M. Montgomery (1981) 'Adult-child discourse at home and at school', in P. French and M. MacLure (eds.) *Adult-child Conversation: Studies in Structure and Process*, Croom Helm, London

## Appendix: Intonation

Some of the examples include a representation of intonation, in which case the following conventions apply:

/    Tone unit boundary. Where an utterance consists of only one tone unit, no boundaries are marked.

'    This symbol immediately precedes both prominent and tonic syllables. Prominent syllables take a single digit before the symbol to indicate their relative pitch height. Tonic syllables take two or more digits before the symbol to indicate the onset level, range and direction of significant pitch movement (see 'Pitch Height' below).

↑↓    Shift of pitch range relatively higher or lower than normal for the speaker.

:    Lengthened syllable. The symbol follows the syllable to which it applies.

Pitch Height. The height, direction and range of significant pitch movement is represented by a set of digits corresponding to points on a scale. The pitch range of a speaker is divided into five notional bands, numbered 1–5 from high to low.

The following information is retrievable from this coding:

| Direction of Movement | Halliday (1967) Tones |
|---|---|
| Falling: (e.g. 13, 25) | Tone 1 |
| Rising: (e.g. 31, 43) | Tone 2 |
| Level: (e.g. 33) | Tone 3 |

Fall-Rise: (e.g. 343) or (e.g. 342)         Tone 4 or Tone 2
Rise-Fall: (e.g. 324)                       Tone 5

## Note

The conventions of transcription allow for 5 gradations of pitch height. In talking about pitch height, levels 1 and 2 are considered 'high', whereas levels 4 and 5 are considered 'low'.

Halliday, M.A.K. (1967) *Intonation and Grammar in British English*, Mouton, The Hague

# 4 DEVELOPMENTAL ASPECTS OF COMMUNICATION: YOUNG CHILDREN'S USE OF REFERRING EXPRESSIONS

Hazel C. Emslie and Rosemary J. Stevenson

This chapter is concerned with the ability of young children to use the definite and indefinite articles. The articles are probably one of the commonest devices in English whereby the speaker indicates to his audience the topic he wishes to comment upon. And whether a speaker chooses to say 'a' rather than 'the' is much more subtle than at first appears. These two words are really quite crucial for maintaining coherence in discourse; and the semantic rules that govern their use can only be stated in terms of the social context, not just in lingusitic terms. Of course, as Brown (1973) points out, the choice of which form to use is always made by the speaker, so it is not what the listener actually knows but what the speaker thinks the listener knows that governs their usage. Thus, investigating the ability of young children to use the articles will give us some idea of their ability to monitor the needs of their audience and to maintain a coherent discourse. For both of these skills, the speaker has to make a complicated assessment of his audience's actual knowledge and probable expectations.

This is not the place to go into the numerous linguistic and cognitive factors governing the appropriate usage of the articles (see Hawkins 1978). Instead we will concentrate on two aspects of their use. The first aspect concerns the distinction between specific and non-specific reference; the second, and perhaps more crucial, aspect concerns the notion of shared knowledge. It is not enough to use the definite article when something is specific for the speaker, it must also be specific for the listener as well. Table 4.1 has been adapted from Brown (1973) with somewhat different examples, and shows the relationship between specific and non-specific reference and the knowledge of the speaker and the listener. We will concentrate here on the two left hand cells. The top left hand cell shows some of the situations where the object referred to is specific for both speaker and listener and the definite article can be used. The first example might be used when two people are in a room together and both of them can see the table. The referent here is unique in a given setting. The second example might be used when the speaker has previously referred to a car. The listener can infer from this which particular engine is being referred to. The engine is definite by entailment. The third example refers to what Karttunen (1976) has termed 'discourse referents'. Discourse referents arise when a particular referent has been previously introduced into the discourse and so has become specific for the listener in that context. The bottom left hand cell shows cases where the referent is specific for the speaker but not for the listener and so has to be introduced by the indefinite article. Once introduced, of course, it can then become a discourse referent and can subsequently be referred to using 'the': it has now become specific for the listener as well.

Table 4.1: The Relation Between Definite and Indefinite Forms and Specific and Nonspecific Reference in Speaker and Listener

| | | SPEAKER | |
| | | SPECIFIC | NONSPECIFIC |
|---|---|---|---|
| LISTENER (as conceived by speaker) | SPECIFIC | DEFINITE: 'the' Where should we put the table? The engine began to make a funny noise 'Discourse Referents' (Karttunen) | NONDEFINITE 'a' Didn't you once write a book on tropical agriculture? |
| | NON-SPECIFIC | NONDEFINITE 'a' I heard a strange noise last night. John tried to buy a house yesterday. | NONDEFINITE 'a' Draw a flower. I haven't got a television. |

As far as the studies we will talk about are concerned, the notion of discourse referents is the most relevant. Consider the following example:

We found a stray dog yesterday.
So we took the dog to the RSPCA.

If a child introduces the referent, 'dog', with 'the' rather than 'a' then it is usually assumed that the child is egocentric (e.g. Piaget 1932). If the child uses the indefinite article on second or subsequent mentions of the dog, this is a coherence failure; he has not made it clear that he is still talking about the same dog.

We can now ask, therefore, when young children acquire both of these skills. The evidence that is available from English speaking subjects is conflicting. Brown's (1973) observations of Adam, Eve and Sarah suggest that usage of the articles becomes stable by the age of three or four, and that at this stage, children rarely make errors of coherence, but they make a large number of egocentric errors, as in the following example:

Sarah:   The cat's dead.
Mother: What cat?

Maratsos (1976) carried out a series of experiments on three- and four-year-old children which essentially enlarged upon Brown's natural-istic data. In one series of experiments, Maratsos told the children some stories and then asked them a question at the end of each story. The results showed that the three-year-olds were very good at producing answers which required the indefinite article, but their performance dropped on answers requiring the definite article. They failed, therefore, to maintain coherence. This was probably due to memory difficulties, and that is essentially how Maratsos interprets the finding. Maratsos found that the four-year-old children fell into two groups. One group (the four-low group) was very good on answers requiring the definite article, but much poorer on answers requiring the indefinite article: their responses were egocentric. The four-high group performed well on both types of answers: they appeared to have mastered the non-egocentric use of the articles.

The data of Warden (1976) contrast sharply with these findings. In one experiment (experiment three), for example, children were given three picture cartoons, and each subject had to tell the story depicted in the cartoons to another subject who could not see the drawings. The most striking result concerned the choice of article for introducing a new referent. Only the adults and the nine-year-old children used reliably more indefinite than definite articles. The younger age groups were inconsistent in their usage. Warden concluded, there-fore, that the non-egocentric use of the articles is not mastered until the age of about nine years.

Our experiments used the same procedure as Warden.[1] There were four groups of ten subjects: parents, four-year-olds, three-year-olds and two-year-olds. Each age group consisted of five pairs of subjects who took it in turns to tell a three picture cartoon story to their partner. The subjects came predominantly from upper working class or middle class backgrounds. The experiments took place in a corridor of the play group which the children attended. The subjects sat one each side of a table, separated by a screen which prevented them from seeing each other's pictures. The screen, though, was adjustable so that the subjects could always see the tops of their partners' heads. The instructions emphasised that the listeners could not see and had never seen their partners' pictures. The pictures were presented to the speakers one at a time, since a pilot study had shown that the younger children had difficulty when all three pictures were presented simultaneously and they tended to concentrate only on the last one. All the responses were tape recorded.

For all three of the experiments we will report here, the basic expectations were as follows. The two-year-old group should include children who were either just acquiring the use of the articles or had not had the use of the articles very long. Hence we would expect them to be fairly inconsistent in their usage. On the basis of Maratsos's findings, we might expect the three-year-old group to produce mainly indefinite articles, even on second mention of a referent. Our design, though, is more like Warden's and from his data we would expect the three-year-olds to produce egocentric responses, using the definite article to introduce a new referent. The four-year-olds should also be egocentric on the basis of Warden's data; while on the basis of Maratsos's data, at least some of the four-year-olds should have mastered the non-egocentric use of the articles. We would expect the adult controls to use the articles appropriately throughout, as Warden's adult group did.

In the first experiment, two cartoon stories were used, one story for each member of the subject pairs. The two stories may be described as follows:

| Story A: | Picture one | A girl is holding a teddy bear and a dog is watching her. |
| | Picture two | The dog is running away with the teddy bear. |
| | Picture three | The girl is running after the dog who has dropped the teddy bear. |
| Story B: | Picture one | A boy and a girl are fishing by a river. |
| | Picture two | The girl has fallen into the river and the boy is looking shocked. |
| | Picture three | The boy is helping the girl out of the river. |

Table 4.2 shows the proportions of referring expressions used for referents mentioned more than once. All subjects used the indefinite

article to introduce the referents. This seems to indicate that even though the objects were specific for the speakers, they were aware that their listeners did not share their knowledge. However, to be really sure that the children are taking the needs of the listener into account, we need to know whether they respond differently to the second mention of a referent as opposed to the first mention. The data for second mention of the referents is shown in the right hand side of Table 4.2. Only the two-year-olds failed to show a reliable preference for the definite article. The three- and four-year-olds, therefore, seem to be sensitive to the need for coherence in discourse and vary their use of the articles depending on whether the information is new or old for the listener.

Table 4.2: Proportions of Referring Expressions used for Referents Mentioned Twice (Experiment 1)

|  | | 1st Mention | |
| --- | --- | --- | --- |
|  | DEFINITE | INDEFINITE | UNDETERM. |
| Parents | — | 0.88 | 0.12 |
| 4-year-olds | 0.04 | 0.96 | — |
| 3-year-olds | — | 0.96 | 0.04 |
| 2-year-olds | — | 0.83 | 0.17 |
|  | | 2nd Mention | |
| Parents | 0.88 | 0.04 | 0.08 |
| 4-year-olds | 1.00 | — | — |
| 3-year-olds | 0.96 | 0.04 | — |
| 2-year-olds | 0.66 | 0.17 | 0.17 |

Perhaps one reason for the greater frequency of indefinite articles in the two-year-olds was because these children did not realise that the referents in the three pictures were the same. Some of the indefinite references for second mention in the other age groups suggest that this might be the case. The second experiment, therefore, was designed to investigate this possibility. The subjects saw all three pictures before they began to tell their story (one picture at a time), to ensure that they recognised the connection between the pictures.

A second aim of experiment two was to investigate the effect of introducing a new referent in the third picture of the cartoon story. In this first experiment, the third picture of story B showed a fish biting the girl's foot. Although only six subjects referred to the fish, two of them (a three-year-old and a four-year-old) used a definite reference, although it obviously had not been mentioned before. It is possible here that as the story progresses, the actual story telling task interferes with the discourse requirements, and the needs of the listener may be temporarily forgotten. In the second experiment, therefore, a new referent, which was an integral part of the story, was introduced into the third picture of each story, in order to examine the above possibility.

The two stories that were used may be described as follows:

| | | |
|---|---|---|
| Story C: | Picture one | A woman and a little girl are standing beside a table. The little girl is reaching for a bottle of milk. |
| | Picture two | The little girl has dropped the bottle of milk and is kneeling on the floor beside the broken bottle. The woman has her hands to her mouth. |
| | Picture three | The little girl is kneeling on the floor and a cat is drinking the milk from the broken bottle. |
| Story D: | Picture one | A boy and a girl are playing with a ball outside a house. |
| | Picture two | The boy has kicked the ball and broken a window in the house. The boy has fallen and the girl is pointing at the broken window. |
| | Picture three | A man is chasing the boy who is running away. |

Table 4.3: Proportions of Referring Expressions used for Referents Mentioned Twice (Experiment 2)

| | 1st Mention | | |
|---|---|---|---|
| | DEFINITE | INDEFINITE | UNDETERM. |
| Parents | 0.13 | 0.83 | 0.04 |
| 4-year-olds | 0.12 | 0.88 | — |
| 3-year-olds | 0.11 | 0.72 | 0.17 |
| 2-year-olds | 0.17 | 0.60 | 0.33 |
| | 2nd Mention | | |
| Parents | 1.00 | — | — |
| 4-year-olds | 1.00 | — | — |
| 3-year-olds | 1.00 | — | — |
| 2-year-olds | 0.60 | 0.20 | 0.20 |

Table 4.3 shows the proportion of definite and indefinite references used to introduce and subsequently refer to all referents that were mentioned more than once. On first mention, all age groups produced

a reliably greater proportion of indefinite articles; and on second mention only the two-year-olds showed no reliable tendency to use a definite reference. The 100 per cent use of definite references by the other groups supports the suggestion that the few errors that they made in the previous experiment were due to their not recognising the connection between the pictures. Seeing all the pictures beforehand, though, did not seem to help the two-year-olds, so it seems reasonable to assume that they were unable to use the definite article to maintain cohesion. It is likely that the task, itself, was rather difficult for them.

Table 4.4: Frequencies of Referring Expressions used to Introduce the New Referent in Picture 3 (cat/man) (Experiment 2)

|  | DEFINITE | INDEFINITE | UNDETERM. |
|---|---|---|---|
| Parents | 7 | 3 | — |
| 4-year-olds | 3 | 5 | — |
| 3-year-olds | 3 | 3 | 3 |
| 2-year-olds | 1 | 6 | 1 |

Table 4.4 shows the frequency of referring expressions used to introduce the new referents (cat/man) in the third pictures. There were no reliable differences in the choice of referring expression, although it is notable that the parents had the highest frequency of definite references, possibly because they had assumed that the cat and the man could be inferred from the context of the story together with plausible assumptions about the world. Perhaps the subjects who used the definite article were demonstrating one of the more subtle uses of 'the' that we normally take for granted.

The third experiment was designed to investigate this possibility by introducing a referent into the third picture which had no connection with the general context or with the previous referents of the story. Another aspect of the third experiment was to introduce a group of students in addition to the parent control group. This was because in experiments one and two, the parents' performance was never better than that of the four-year-olds when introducing a referent. In his experiments, Warden used students as his adult controls and they always performed with 100 per cent accuracy. Perhaps students do not perform in quite the same way as parents in these experiments.

The stories in experiment three may be described as follows:

Story E:   Picture one   A man is sitting at a table and a waiter is bringing him some food.

| | | |
|---|---|---|
| | Picture two | The waiter spills the food over the man. |
| | Picture three | The man is wiping the food off his clothes. A clown is juggling with three balls. |
| Story F: | Picture one | A man is sitting in a railway carriage and a girl is putting a suitcase onto the rack. |
| | Picture two | The man is reading and the suitcase is falling onto the girl's head. |
| | Picture three | The girl is rubbing her head. A horse is looking through the window. |

Table 4.5: Proportions of Referring Expressions used for Referents Mentioned Twice (Experiment 3)

| | | 1st Mention | |
|---|---|---|---|
| | DEFINITE | INDEFINITE | UNDETERM. |
| Students | — | 1.00 | — |
| Parents | 0.13 | 0.87 | — |
| 4-year-olds | 0.12 | 0.88 | — |
| 3-year-olds | 0.13 | 0.83 | 0.04 |
| | | 2nd Mention | |
| Students | 1.00 | — | — |
| Parents | 0.97 | — | 0.03 |
| 4-year-olds | 1.00 | — | — |
| 3-year-olds | 1.00 | — | — |

Table 4.5 shows the proportions of referring expressions that were used to introduce and subsequently refer to all referents that were mentioned more than once. (Two-year-olds were not included in this experiment.) The pattern is now familiar. All age groups reliably used the articles appropriately, although the parents were not quite as accurate as either the students or the four-year-olds.

Table 4.6: Frequencies of Referring Expressions used to Introduce the Incongruous Referent (horse/clown) in Picture 3 (Experiment 3)

| | DEFINITE | INDEFINITE | UNDETERM. |
|---|---|---|---|
| Students | 0 | 10 | 0 |
| Parents | 0 | 10 | 0 |
| 4-year-olds | 1 | 9 | 0 |
| 3-year-olds | 2 | 7 | 1 |

Table 4.6 shows the frequencies of referring expressions used to introduce the incongruous referents (horse/clown) in the third pictures. Only the three-year-olds showed no reliable tendency to use the indefinite more often than the definite article. This suggests that in the previous experiment, at least for the four-year-olds and adults, the use of the definite article was based on assumptions about the listener's knowledge.

The findings of this series of experiments have several implications. First, we seem to have found that from the age of three, young children have mastered the non-egocentric use of the articles, and seem sensitive to discourse requirements. This non-egocentric usage is contrary to the findings of Maratsos with some of his four-year-olds and of Warden for children under nine. These differences are most likely due to differences in task (Maratsos) and materials (Warden). (See Clark and Clark 1977: 369 for an example of Warden's stories.) It is also possible that some of Warden's subjects were telling their stories to the experimenter, who knew the pictures, rather than to their partners.

Secondly, the two-year-olds seem unable to maintain discourse coherence through the use of the definite article. They behave rather like Maratsos's three-year-old group. It seems likely that (among other things) they had memory or perceptual difficulties which prevented them from recognising identical referents in different pictures. Presumably this tendency occurred earlier in our studies than in Maratsos's because the memory load was greater in the story tasks of Maratsos.

Thirdly, the new referents in the third pictures of experiment two seemed to lead some speakers to assume that the identity of the man and the cat could be inferred from the story context and general knowledge. This tendency disappeared with the four-year-olds and adults in experiment three where the new referents could not be related to the stories. The extent to which speakers made those assumptions in experiment two, though, was very variable, and it seems likely that there are quite large individual differences in the assumptions a speaker will make about what the listener can infer.

And finally, the parent control group was never as accurate as the four-year-olds, while the student group was 100 per cent accurate in experiment three. We suggest that parents are the most appropriate adult group to use in these kinds of experiments. We suspect, though, that students also have failures of communication outside the experimental setting. We plan to collect some naturalistic data on adults to compare with the kinds of errors Brown observed in his children. We strongly suspect that there will be at least as many errors.

## Note

1. For details of the experimental procedures, see Emslie & Stevenson (in preparation).

## References

Brown, R. (1973) *A First Language: The Early Stages*, Harvard University Press, Cambridge, Mass.

Clark, H.H. & E.V. Clark (1977) *Psychology and Language: An Introduction to Psycholinguistics*, Harcourt Brace Jovanovich

Emslie, H.C. & R.J. Stevenson (in preparation) 'Preschool children's use of the articles in definite and indefinite referring expressions'

Hawkins, J. (1978) *Definiteness and Indefiniteness: A Study in Reference and Grammaticality Prediction*, Croom Helm, London

Karttunen, L. (1976) 'Discourse Referents', in J.D. McCawley (ed.) *Syntax and Semantics, 7,* Academic Press, New York

Maratsos, M.P. (1976) *The Use of Definite and Indefinite Reference in Young Children*, Cambridge University Press, Cambridge

Piaget, J. (1932) *The Language and Thought of the Child*, 2nd edn, Kegan, Paul, Trench, Trubner & Co., London

Warden, D.A. (1976) 'The influence of context on children's use of identifying expressions and references', *British Journal of Psychology, 67,* 101-12

Part Two

THEORY AND ANALYSIS

# 5 CONVERSATIONAL UNITS AND THE USE OF 'WELL...'

Marion Owen

## Introduction

The first version of this paper (Owen 1979) was originally written in order to elucidate certain questions that were arising in the study of 'remedial interchanges' (cf. Goffman 1971: Ch. 4): those exchanges involving — in English — apologies, accounts, and the responses made to them. The formulation of a research topic in such terms implied the existence of at least one kind of internally coherent unit of conversation, the **interchange**, which is itself built up out of smaller units. We therefore began to examine a wider range of conversational material (consisting of naturally-occurring, tape-recorded talk) in order to establish just what the 'building blocks' of conversation are. The first section of this paper is a brief summary of the treatment of **turns** and **moves** given in Owen (1979); much of the work of other researchers described there is by now becoming familiar and is widely available in published form (e.g. Schegloff: 1968, Sacks, Schegloff and Jefferson: 1974). In the subsequent sections we deal first with larger conversational units, and then provide an analysis of the use of 'well', which we hope illustrates the value of this approach. Finally we consider the relationship between conversational units and the linguistic entities known as **sentences**.

## Turns and moves

In our earlier paper Owen (1979) we adopted by and large the now classic treatment of turns and turn-taking given by Sacks, Schegloff and Jefferson (1974). However, we gave additional consideration to the problem of just what stretches of talk by one speaker can count as turns. In the first place, we distinguish turns proper from **back-channel utterances** (cf. Duncan and Niederehe 1974) which, far from being attempts to take the floor, actually ratify the continuing speaker's right to hold it. Back-channel utterances take forms such as 'mmhm', 'uhhuh', and 'yeah'; Schegloff (1968:380) calls them 'demonstrations of continued, co-ordinated hearership' and points out that they are not heard as 'interruptions' in spite of being produced simultaneously with another's talk.

Sacks, Schegloff and Jefferson (1974) label the point at which speaker change can occur as a **transition-relevance place** (TRP). They observe that TRPs occur at 'possible completion points' of 'sentences, clauses, phrases, and one-word constructions, and multiples thereof' (1974:721), but since they acknowledge that features such as intonation will have to be taken into account they recognise that their account is only a partial one. The occurrence of TRPs can account for some examples of overlap between turns, as in the following example:[1]

> (1) Salesman:    we can ˈfix you ˈup | we ˈhave got them ˈboth in
> ˌstock // | ˈtwo ˈthree ˈfour | ˈand ˈtwo ˈthree
> ˌfive‖
>
> Customer:    you ˌhave got them ˑboth in ˑstock | oh ˆhave
> you // | ˈthat's ˌsomething‖
>
> Salesman:    ˌyes‖

Two instances of overlap occur here; in both cases the 'second' speaker begins at a possible completion point during the 'first' speaker's turn. We suspect, however, that even a syntactic-prosodic account of TRPs must give way to some kind of functional explanation; in our terms this could take the form of a requirement that a **turn** must contain at least one **move**.

We take the term **move** from Goffman (1976:272) where he defines the unit as 'any full stretch of talk or of its substitutes which has a distinctive unitary bearing on some set or other of the circumstances in which the participants find themselves'. A turn may, under various conditions, contain more than one move.[2] For example, data published in Owen (1979) shows how a speaker may preface his turn with a phrase such as 'first of all', indicating that a list will follow; his addressee should therefore not take the first apparent completion point as an opportunity to take the floor. In a sense such phrases create from the material they preface a single 'super-move' in which smaller components can be identified.

A turn may also contain the second part of one adjacency pair[3] and the first of another; the most obvious ordering of such structures is as follows:

> (2) Customer:    ˈyou've ˈsold ˆout of ˑListeners | ˌhave you‖

Shopkeeper: yes I'm ˅terribly ˙sorry ˙dear | ˙we ˋhave‖ ˋis there ˙something ˅special ˙in it ˙this ˙week‖

In this example the shopkeeper's turn consists of (at least) two moves:[4] one, positioned first, responds to the customer's question, and the second initiates a second adjacency pair. Other arrangements are possible, however:

(3)  A: hel͵lo | ˈcan I ͵help you‖
     B: oh ˈhel͵lo | ͵yes‖

This has the following structure:

A:  [greeting]    –    [offer]
        ↓                  ↓
B:  [greeting]    –    [acceptance]

Turns are thus **structural** units into which **functional** units – moves – are slotted. The turn-taking system described by Sacks, Schegloff and Jefferson (1974) is functionally motivated, since speaker change can be shown to depend on the type of moves being made: for example, speaker change 'should' occur immediately after a question (in that its absence will be noticeable to participants and analysts alike), whereas following an assessment or evaluation the requirement for a response still operates but is less powerful.

## Larger Units

Analysis of data demonstrates that it is often necessary to look beyond a single turn in order to analyse it into its component moves, and to establish what those moves are. The use of terms such as 'response', 'answer', 'adjacency pair' and 'exchange' implies that moves are part of larger functional units of some kind. The adjacency pair is in fact the smallest of these, defined (in terms of utterances) by Schegloff and Sacks (1973:238) as a sequence of two utterances produced by different speakers, one immediately following the other, and tied together in a special way which is 'partially the product of the operation of a typology in the speakers' production of the sequences'. Thus utterance types can be divided into 'first pair-parts' and 'second pair-parts' such as QUESTION/ANSWER, OFFER/ACCEPTANCE or

OFFER/REFUSAL. Three-part exchanges are also possible, such as COMPLAINT/APOLOGY/ACCEPTANCE, in which the middle component acts both as a second pair-part to the first component and a first pair-part to the last.

However, it is not utterances that are tied together to form adjacency pairs, but moves. Goffman (1976:259) provides the following example:

> (4)  A: have you got coffee to go?
>       B: milk and sugar?
>       A: just milk

If we search B's turn for an answer to A's question, we conclude that the unstated answer must be 'yes', since otherwise B's question would be irrelevant. B's turn can thus be treated as containing a conflation of two moves, giving us two adjacency pairs within only three turns and three utterances. Similarly in extract (2) above, three adjacency pairs can be found within three turns.[5] We even find what the grammarian would call 'self-embedding', where the nested structure is of the same type as the matrix pair: QUESTION/ANSWER nested in QUESTION/ANSWER is particularly common. Such patternings Jefferson (1972) calls 'side-sequences', and the following extract illustrates this:

> (5)  $C_1$: 'would you 'rather I 'wrote a ˌchequeǁ
>       $S_1$: ˌyeahǁ you 'got a ˅card I ˙s'pose | a ˅banker's ˙cardǁ
>       $C_2$: 'yes I ˌhave | ˌyesǁ
>       $S_2$: yes I 'think ˙so | in ˌthis ˙caseǁ

The pair structure of (5) is not quite as clear-cut as in the imaginary data often constructed, since the salesman answers the question in $C_1$ — provisionally perhaps — before inserting the first part of an embedded QUESTION/ANSWER pair. Nevertheless, (5) has the structure:

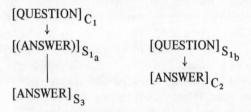

To understand the last move in structures like these, participants and analyst must recognise it as the second part of an adjacency pair. However, as it is not positioned immediately after its first pair-part, we have to look back through the conversation to find the question to which it is an answer. It is therefore often necessary to take a unit larger than two adjacent moves – in this case, a four-part **interchange** – in order to make sense of one particular utterance. In principle, there is no limit on how much may be inserted between a question and its answer, though some adjacency pairs – APOLOGY/ACCEPTANCE, for example – nearly always *are* actually adjacent; it is as yet an open question as to what kinds of pairs may be split up in this way, and what kinds of pairs may be inserted into the 'gap' thus created.

The recognition of conversational units beyond moves and turns can on occasion reveal properties of individual moves. Consider the following data:

(6)  Student$_1$ :  I'm ˇvery ·sorry I ·have to ˇgo‖
     Lecturer$_1$ :  not at ˋall‖
     Student$_2$ :  ((smiling)) I ˇmean ˌthat‖

Why should the student say $S_2$ as a rejoinder to $L_1$? Expressions of regret are standardly used as ritual apologies, in which the speaker need not 'literally' mean what he says for the utterance to be a success-ful performance of 'apologising'.[6] But this, of course, does not preclude the 'sincere' expression of regret. L responds to $S_1$ as a ritual apology; if this were not the case, we would have to understand $L_1$ as a very curious denial of the genuine nature of S's reported feelings. S points out, and plays upon, the potential pragmatic ambiguity[7] of such ritual expressions. Note that in this instance there is a difference between

(7a)  I'm ˇvery ·sorry I ·have to ˇgo‖

for which the 'sincere' reading is more likely, and

(7b)  I'm ˈvery ˇsorry | I ˈhave to ˇgo‖

which would probably be interpreted as a ritual apology. However, (7a) can have either reading, as (6) shows. The examination of larger units as a whole can thus reveal aspects of the nature of their components.

Conversations, then, may be 'chunked' by participants into a series of larger units, which we will call **interchanges**; bracketing by means of an adjacency pair[8] is one way of doing this. All that intervenes between, say, a question and its answer, can be understood as oriented to the topic introduced by the initial question.

Speakers also use specific devices to mark off **sections** or phases of conversations: Schegloff and Sacks (1973) show how closing sequences, particularly in telephone conversations (where the end of the conversation also marks the end of contact between the participants) are initiated in particular ways. One speaker, A, offers a 'possible pre-closing move' which, if accepted by B, becomes the first move of the closing section. Since the utterances used for possible pre-closings (e.g. 'well,' so, "O K) are used for other purposes too, the problem for the addressee is to know when they *are* being used to attempt to initiate a closing section. Schegloff and Sacks find that they 'operate as possible pre-closings when placed at the analysable (once again, to *participants*) end of a topic' (Schegloff and Sacks 1973:247). Another technique involves either participant referring back to the 'reason for calling' after talk on other topics has intervened, as in the following:

(8)  R:  '6 '9 ˌ1 | ·2 ·2 ·6ˌ4||

　　C:  's 'that ˇMichael||

　　R:  ˌyeah||

　　C:  it's `Jane||

　　R:  'helˌlo |ˌJane||

　　C:  'helˌlo | I've got a 'lot of ˌmail ·down ·here | ofˌyours||

　　R:  ˌhave you||

　　C:  ˌyes | but I've ·got my ·big ˇconflict | toˌnight | and I ·just ·can't ·bring it `up hhh|| so if ˆone of you ·wants to ·pop ·down and ˇget it|| I ˆhate to be ˇmean but I (daren't)//I can't

　　R:  it o/it's 'O K | we'll ·pop ·down to`morrow ·Jane||

　　C:  you ˇsure | you ·don't | it ·is an ˆawful 'lot of it | you ˆwant to ·quickly ·nip ·down ˇnow for it||

　　R:  'OˌK | I ˋwill|| er hey | you 'know that er | have 'you been 'lighting a ˋfire ·down ·there||

　　C:  ˌyes||

((topic section 3 min. 20 secs))

　　R:  'oh ˌyes | I mean it's ˆfairly ˇcommon | even in ·sort of ·two ·storey ˋhouses|| ((1.5 secs.)) ˋany ·rate | I'll 'come ˌdown | and er col 'lect this ˌmail||

　　C:  ˌyeah||

((closing section 15 secs))

C: ⸌yeahhhhhhh‖ 'O͵K‖
R: 'O͵K | ˈsee you in a // ͵minute | ͵Jane‖
C: ͵yeah | 'O͵K | ͵right‖ // ⱽbye‖
R: ⱽbye‖

R's utterance 'any rate I'll come down and collect this mail' is an example of what Schegloff and Sacks call a re-invocation. They point out that closing sequences, i.e. those in which a possible pre-closing move is accepted, are 'not a place for new things to come up', though re-invocation, as in (8), may itself lead to other connected topics coming up naturally. Observing, however, that other unrelated topics *are* sometimes brought up in closing sections, Schegloff and Sacks, by pointing out that this must be done with special 'markers', establish that the closing section is a unit to which participants themselves are oriented. Such 'misplacement markers', used elsewhere in conversation as well, include 'by the way', and 'I was going to say . . .'. The latter Schegloff and Sacks call a 'contrast marking', the contrast being with the assumption that new materials do not come up in closing sections.

## An Illustrative Analysis

We have arrived at a four-level hierarchy of units within natural conversation; with the largest first, this is:

| | |
|---|---|
| SECTION | e.g. topic section (functional) |
| ↑ | closing section (structural) |
| INTERCHANGE | e.g. any adjacency pair (structural) |
| ↑ | remedial interchanges (functional) |
| TURN | (structural unit, defined partly in functional |
| ↑ | terms, i.e. excluding back-channel utterances) |
| MOVE | (functional unit, defined partly in structural |
| | terms, e.g. an answer as a second pair-part) |

It is not possible, of course, to give examples of the unit 'turn' in the above list, since this is a unit with a different status from the others. Whereas moves, interchanges and sections are functional or semantic units, the turn is, as we have seen, incidental to these. Nevertheless, it needs to be included in the hierarchy since we can also show how the turn-taking system can affect turn- and thus move-construction. We have already mentioned, for example, how a phrase such as 'first of all' can be used by a speaker at or near the beginning of his turn to establish that it will be constructed as an open-ended list, thus making it more difficult for other participants to take the floor. We have specified (Owen 1979) that a turn, to qualify as such, must consist of at least one move; whether there is an upper limit in ordinary conversation is open to question.

We come now to a demonstration of the application of these conclusions to the analysis of language usage. This will be approached through a critique of just one study which proceeds by constructing sentences and then imagining the contexts in which they might be used appropriately. We have chosen R. Lakoff (1973) simply because it provides some instances of the interesting results that can be reached even without the analysis of 'live' data. We hope to show that the results obtainable by this method are, and perhaps can only be, partial, so that generalisations made on the basis of intuition alone are likely to be inadequate.

Lakoff observes that appropriate responses to questions are of three kinds:

> (i) non-answers e.g. 'none of your business', 'ask John', etc. (We shall not be discussing this type further here.)
> (ii) direct answers e.g. A: what's the time?
> B: three o'clock.
> (iii) indirect answers e.g. A: what's the time?
> B; I just told Bill it was noon/ the milkman's just been, etc.

Type (iii) differs from type (ii) in that assumptions are required over and above 'those entailed by the question itself' (Lakoff 1973:456) to enable B to work out (approximately) what time it is.

Lakoff then notes that type (iii) answers, but not type (ii), may be prefaced by 'well', which is then interpretable as a hedge addressed to Grice's Maxim of Quantity: B knows he is not giving directly the information the questioner sought, but that the answer he does give will allow A to infer that information.

A 'live' example of a type (iii) answer occurs in the following extract:

> (9) A: I 'wonder if you can 'charge it to my deˌpartment | at the uniˇversity | who 'will ˇpay for it‖ ˈif you 'can't I'll 'write you a ˌcheque‖
> B: ˌyeah | well they're exˈtremely good 'discount ˌprices‖

If we allow that (9)A expresses a question, then for (9)B to stand as an answer to that question, A must make an inference based on the common knowledge that charging goods by invoice costs money; the implication is that the shop cannot do this *and* maintain its low prices, so that implied answer to the question is 'no' (an answer which is given explicitly later in the transaction).

Lakoff's second type of context for the appropriate use of 'well' is that in which it 'operates as a signal that the rest of the answer . . . is not to be taken as a complete reply giving all the information necessary'. In this context, 'well' may preface direct (type ii) answers as well, and in fact it is just this co-occurrence that triggers the inference that the answer is incomplete. Lakoff's archetype is:

(10) A: did you kill your wife?
     B: well, yes.

in which B's reply (compare this with a bald 'yes') implies, perhaps, that there were extenuating circumstances. The following seems to be an example:

(11) A: is ¹that all ¹right/I mean if er you've ˋblocked it ·off ·now so it's OˇK‖
     B: er well it's ¹all ¹right up ˇhere | I don't/ er Steve/ I ¹told ¹Steve and ¹Myra to ¹do the ˋsame‖

The implication of B's answer — conveyed also by hesitation and the fall-rise intonation — is that while 'it's all right here' it may not be all right 'somewhere else'.

According to Lakoff, 'well' may also occur with direct answers 'when the reply is directed toward a question other than the overt one' (1973:460), but her example of this seems to fall under the previous type of usage, so we will not discuss it separately here.

Lakoff notes that 'well' occurs not only in rejoinders to questions but also in the questions themselves, in responses to commands, and in responses to simple declaratives' (1973:462), but she predicts that the same conditions govern the use of 'well' in these environments too. Her generalisation is expressed through the notion of 'insufficiency'; in answers, the insufficiency lies in the response prefaced by 'well', whereas in other environments 'it is due to an insufficiency felt by the user of "well" to have occurred in the utterance or action to which his question or, presumably, his command or statement is a response'

(1973:463). Thus to take just one of Lakoff's examples:

> (12) well, didn't it rain yesterday, just like I said it would?

Lakoff claims this is 'a triumphant exclamation, demanding agreement that the speaker was right all the time'. So far, so good, but it is hard to fit this in under the general concept of 'insufficiency'. Presumably what had been lacking here was an admission by the addressee that the speaker's prediction had been correct, but far too much stretching of the notion of insufficiency is necessary in order to accommodate even those examples that Lakoff produces.

Finally, Lakoff mentions 'one other type of "well", found within narratives, that a speaker uses to indicate insufficiency in an utterance of his own'. Typically, this usage precedes 'to cut a long story short . . .'. On this interpretation, 'insufficiency' explains 'well' used before statements, as well as before answers and questions, but the only statements Lakoff considers are those within narratives. Of course, most answers are statements too; there is a confusion here between sentence types and conversational moves.

The questions we wish to raise are these: can the appropriate usage of 'well' be accounted for without the analysis of conversations into units and providing a characterisation of those units as moves, turns, interchanges and sections, then considering the placement of 'well' with respect to these? Secondly, and more generally, can such an approach proceed without the analysis of 'real' conversational materials, or can we continue to rely on intuition alone?

In an attempt to answer these questions we have adopted the following method:

1. Take a corpus of tape-recorded conversations and locate occurrences of 'well', limiting the scope (as Lakoff does for the most part) to those at or very near the beginnings of turns.
2. Limit the scope further to instances of 'well' which preface the second pair-part of an adjacency pair.
3. Identify the nature of the moves preceding and following 'well'.
4. Compare the environments in which 'well' does occur with similar environments in which it does not.
5. Look for a pattern or generalisation.

In steps 1 to 3 of this procedure, it was found that 'well' was used to preface the second part of these types of adjacency pairs:

## 1. ASSESSMENT – DISAGREEMENT/QUALIFIED AGREEMENT

(13) A: . . . because 'some 'records are 'rather ex˅pensive | ˋaren't
·they‖

B: well they ˋall are | in a ˅way‖

(14) A₁: they 'must ˅worry a·bout you ·though | ·Eddie | ʹdon't
·they‖ your ˌMum and ˌDad | ˌwhen you're ˌdoing ˌall
these ˌjumps‖

B₁: er well they 'always 'come to ˋall the ˌshows‖

A₂: ˌdo they‖

B₂: ˌyeah | and ·they en˅joy it‖

(15) A: 'do you not 'think that you 'might be en˅couraging
·people to have ·sex at a ·much ·earlier ·age‖

B: well by sug'gesting that the 'age of con'sent ·should be
re'duced to four'teen | I 'don't 'think we're ˅doing ·that‖

The A-moves in these examples all present an assessment which B might accept; in (13), B modifies the assessment, and in (14) and (15) B rejects it altogether.

## 2. QUESTION – RESPONSE, *where the response cancels a presupposition of the question*

(16) A: 'any i'dea when he's/

B: well he's 'not 'likely to 'be a 'round | 'not 'really to˅morrow
| ˋeither | he ·doesn't ˅think‖

(Types 1 and 2 are closely related.)

## 3. REQUEST – NON-COMPLIANCE

(17) A: 'can I 'just ˌsee them‖

B: ˊum | well I'm 'not al'lowed to | to ·do ˌthat‖

(Another example occurs in extract (9))

## 4. OFFER – REJECTION

(18) A: 'what a'bout 'coming 'here on the ˌway | or or 'doesn't
that 'give you e'nough ˌtime‖

B: well ˌno | I'm 'supervising ˋhere‖

Some of these results are supported by independent studies. Pomerantz (1975, 1977), for example, found that one prevalent turn organisation when agreement is invited is the prefaced disagreement, with 'uh', 'well', etc., preceding the stated disagreement (1977:18). Wootton (forthcoming), in a study of grantings and rejections of children's requests by their parents, shows that 'well' is used before non-grantings, but not before granting moves.

The fact that the same strategy can be used to preface four types of second pair-parts, and is used much less with their 'positive' counterparts, clearly suggests that these move-types have something in common. Pomerantz and Wootton, having demonstrated the different turn-constructions displayed by disagreements and non-grantings, contrasted with the construction of agreements and grantings, argue that turns are constructed so as to exhibit a preference[9] for agreements and grantings. Wootton concludes, however, that

> there may be very general ways through which such preferences are displayed, ways which are, in some sense, non-sequence type specific, but at this stage, given the limited number of detailed sequential analyses, it is probably premature to attempt a formal statement of these ways (ibid.)

At this point Wootton refers in a footnote to a candidate for such a 'formal statement' the study of politeness strategies by Brown and Levinson (1978), in which the authors develop the notion of **face** (borrowed from oriental cultures by Goffman (1967)). Face can be defined briefly as 'the public self-image that every member wants to claim for himself' (Brown and Levinson 1978:66) which, since it cannot be naturally maintained by ego, depends on mutual co-operation between ego and alter, each maintaining the other's face. In terms of this model, certain conversational moves — including the second pair-parts in (13)–(18) — can be described as threats to alter's face, and it then becomes possible to explain some of the regularities observable in linguistic usage as strategies oriented to the preservation of face. Thus we can describe 'well', used to preface a second pair-part which is also a face-threatening act, as a strategy for signalling that a face-threat is about to occur, thereby giving attention to alter's face and reducing the subsequent threat. This interpretation accounts partially for Lakoff's intuition that 'well' precedes indirect answers, not because indirectness is face-threatening in itself, but rather because it is just those moves that are face-threatening that are often performed indirectly. The co-occurrence observable between 'well' and some indirect answers is thus a second-order regularity. Extract (9) supports this account since, although it is an indirect answer, it functions as a rejection of a request and is thus face-threatening.

It should be stressed that linguistic regularities of this kind are not —

unlike the regularities of syntax — appropriately described as the output of *rules*. In all the contexts in question there are alternative, and usually equally effective, strategies; one of these is hesitation or delay, display-ing reluctance or the problematic nature of the forthcoming move (discussed also by Wootton and Pomerantz), which is sometimes used in conjunction with 'well', as in extracts (14) and (17). It is worth noting in this connection that Good (1978) and Good and Butterworth (1978) argue that hesitation phenomena may not always be simple indicators of the speaker's cognitive load, directly accountable for in terms of the complexity of the task involved in formulating the utterance, but that speakers can *use* hesitancy as a means for achieving an interactional goal 'even though the difficulty of the particular utterance would not directly necessitate the change' (Good and Butterworth 1978:1). Speakers thus have a way of communicating (i.e. conveying intentionally) that the forthcoming utterance is problematic for them. The notion of 'difficulty' as used by Good and Butterworth, where it refers to cog-nitive load, may be extendable into the domain of face-preservation and face-threatening behaviour. We might then interpret 'well', like hesitation phenomena, as (in this environment) one of a set of strategies available to speakers for communicating 'difficulty'.

Another interesting use of 'well' before second pair-parts seems to be only partially accountable for in terms of this model. Example (5) above contains a 'side-sequence', the archetypal structure of which is:

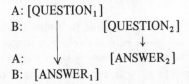

A: [QUESTION₁]
B:                    [QUESTION₂]
                          ↓
A:        ↓        [ANSWER₂]
B:   [ANSWER₁]

where the inserted question/answer pair is topically related to the outer pair, often clearing up some point which must be established before an answer to the first question can be provided. Extract (19) contains another example:

(19) A: ˈroughly ˈhow many ˌpagesǁ
   B: ˊumǁ well ˈcould/ | ˈletˈs ˈsee | ˋcould you ·do them in ·such
        a ·way that it would be ·printed on ·A  four |
   A: ⌈ˈA  four | ˌrightǁ
   B: ⌊·but  folded | ·so that it would ˋcome ·down to ·A ˇfiveǁ
   A: ˌyes | ˈwhat ˈsort of ˌquantityǁ

B: well in ¹that ¹case I would ¹think a¹bout ¹fifty ₚsheets ǀ
per·haps‖

This has the following move structure:

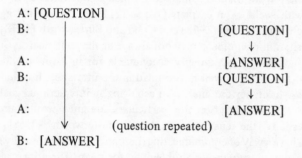

A: [QUESTION]
B:                                          [QUESTION]
                                                ↓
A:                                          [ANSWER]
B:                                          [QUESTION]
                                                ↓
A:                                          [ANSWER]
                        (question repeated)
B:  [ANSWER]

It is quite common to find 'well' inserted by B at the beginning and end
of a side-sequence, often with 'in that case' or 'then' coupled with the
second occurrence. Given the normal preference for an answer to follow
the question immediately, it would be possible to interpret 'well' as a
marker of the disjunctions occurring when a side-sequence is inserted.
However, to describe both these disjunctions, 'caused' by B, as threats
to A's face, seems implausible, although the first could perhaps be seen
in this light. The second 'well' is particularly problematic in the case of
(19), since the question is repeated, so that no disjunction occurs.

Clearly more remains to be said about the distribution and functions
even of an apparently simple item like 'well', but to return to the
questions raised earlier: the account given here of 'well' as a strategy
for prefacing face-threatening second pair-parts can only be expressed —
indeed the problem can only be defined — in terms of the units of
conversation introduced in the previous section. The answer to the
second question is more a matter of conviction, and perhaps cannot be
proven, but we believe that results of this kind can only be achieved
through the detailed analysis of real conversations.

### 'Conversational Units' and 'Sentences'

It cannot be too strongly emphasised that the examples provided here
of 'moves' cannot be identified with 'sentences' or even 'sentence-types':
they are, by contrast, interactional units. As Schegloff points out
(1976) for example, not all moves that are syntactically in question-form

function interactionally as questions, and not all interactional questions have syntactic question-form. This is not to say that there is no connection at all between the two. Schegloff (1976:32) suggests that linguistic form may have 'constraint-meeting power'; that is, given an independent sequential basis for finding an utterance to be a question 'if one can' (the last being the constraint), that constraint can be met by the linguistic form of the utterance — its interrogative form'. (It would be useful to talk only of interrogatives when in the domain of syntax and reserve 'question' as a term for an interactional move which happens — usually — to be accomplished by linguistic means.) Such a conclusion, if correct, should warn us against the widespread belief that linguistic analysis, having begun with isolated sentences, can, *retaining the same methods*, widen its domain to the study of conversation. For the way in which this is usually attempted is to construct an isolated sentence and then to surround it with equally imaginary 'contexts', linguistic and otherwise, to see how these might contribute to its 'situated meaning'.[10] Such an approach is concerned with problems like 'how the ideal speaker-hearer uses sentences of the language to communicate propositions that are not senses of these sentences in the language' (Katz 1977:20); for example, how can a sentence with assertion form come to be uttered with question meaning? Questions like this are misleading, however, in that they imply that 'meanings in context' have the same status as sentence-meanings. Within a model of this kind, problems like 'how does this utterance function as an answer/pre-closing move/complaint?' cannot even be raised, because answers, complaints and the like are interactional, not grammatical units, and can only be understood by examining real conversations to see how they are structured and organised by the participants themselves. As Schegloff (1976:47) puts it,

> Taking sentences in isolation is not just a matter of taking such sentences that might appear *in* a context *out* of the context . . . the very composition, construction, assemblage of the sentences is predicated by their speakers on the place in which it is being produced, and it is through *that* that a sentence is context-bound, rather than possibly independent sentences being different intact objects in or out of context.

This type of analysis challenges the grammarian's traditional context-independent approach to a typology of utterances: 'Finding an utterance to be an "answer" . . . cannot be achieved by reference to phonological, syntactic, semantic or logical features of the utterance itself, but only by consulting its sequential placement, e.g. its placement "after a question"' (Schegloff and Sacks 1973:241-2). To this challenge the grammarian may reply that he is concerned with the analysis not of utterances, but sentences, and would not attempt to predict that any particular sentence or sentence-type could be used to accomplish 'answering'. For Katz: 'Sentence meaning is the meaning of a sentence type *in the language*, whereas utterance meaning is the meaning of a particular use, or token, of a sentence-type *on that particular occasion*.' (1977:14, original emphasis).

It is thus not part of the grammarian's task to predict that a sentence such as

(20) were you brought up in a barn?

can be used, in appropriate circumstances, as a directive to the addressee telling him to shut the door. All the grammarian has to say about (20) is that it has an interrogative form, and that it is an enquiry about the addressee's upbringing. It is left to a pragmatic theory —for Katz and others, part of 'performance' — to describe how (20) might be used. Pragmatics thus describes how properties of the language system interact with properties of context to derive 'situated meanings'. There is, however, an assumption in this reply, which is that context-independent grammar can and will have at least something to say about the properties of all utterances taken in isolation, or that any utterance functioning as a conversational move derives at least some of its situated meaning from properties of the language itself. While this assumption may be strictly valid for all purely linguistic utterances, we find if we examine real conversations that in many cases an utterance derives so little of its 'meaning' from the language, and so much from the context, including its structural placement, that a sentence grammar can have virtually nothing to contribute to an understanding of it.

For example: no grammarian, to our knowledge, has ever proposed that laughter should or could be treated as part of a grammar, and yet laughter can undoubtedly function as a conversational move, as in the following example:

(21) A: . . . I •actually `push | the •aircraft ‚out | and er it •seems
        •such a •shame (----------) to •run it `down‖
     B: `you're •not the •guy •down •there who ˇkick-starts 'em
        •are you‖

A: ⁻er ˇno | I er 'you ˌknow‖
B: hhhhhhh
A: oh ˋkick-start 'em | I'm ˇsorry | I ·didn't ˋget ˌthat‖ 'heh 'heh
   'heh‖

A fails to 'get' B's joke, and B's laugh functions partly as a move
explaining his previous turn, as if to say 'there was a joke there, and if
you find it you'll be able to make sense of what I said'. B thus utilises
A's knowledge of the structural placement of laughter − informally,
the fact that people laugh *at* things − to explain his own utterance to
A. The conversational functions of laughter have been extensively
studied by Jefferson (forthcoming), who has demonstrated the sequential
consequences for a conversation of the production of laughter. In (21),
for example, A could not have produced his third turn without B's
intervening laughter.

A sentence grammar within any model cannot, as far as we can see,
account for the conversational role of laughter. More generally, it is
ill-equipped for the description of phenomena whose nature is closely
bound up with their sequential placement, such as the unfolding,
developing, structures of natural conversations.


## Notes

1. We use the following notation for intonation and other features:
(a) *Intonation*: nuclear marks:
ˌlow fall; ˌlow rise; ˋhigh fall; ˊhigh rise; ˇ fall-rise; ˆ rise-fall.
ı 'prominent stress; ·non-prominent stress.
⁻ ⁻high or mid-level pitch.
‖ | major and minor tone-group boundaries.
(b) *Other notation*:
// point during a turn at which second speaker begins
/ 'self-interruption'

{ simultaneous speech by two or more speakers

(------------) indecipherable passage
(words) unclear passage
2. This possibility is recognised by Schegloff (1968:351) who talks of activities.
3. For this term, see the following section, and Schegloff and Sacks (1973).
4. A more detailed analysis of this extract is presented in Owen (1979). We
propose there that the shopkeeper's first major intonational tone group in fact
contains an APOLOGY move 'nested' into an ANSWERING move.
5. Extract (21) below displays a more complex pair structure still, in that A's
laughter in response to B's joke does not appear until after a sequence analysable
as two adjacency pairs has been inserted. See Owen (1979).
6. Cf. Owen (1980:177−81) for a discussion of the 'sincerity problem' in the
speech act analysis of apologies.

7. Cf. Weiser (1974).
8. We will retain this term, though it is not strictly applicable to pairs that are not temporally adjacent.
9. For discussion of this technical sense of 'preference' see Owen (1980:212-18).
10. We interpret speech act theory as essentially a variant of this approach.

# References

Brown, P. and S.C. Levinson (1978) 'Universals in Language Usage: Politeness Phenomena' in E. Goody (ed.), *Questions and Politeness: Strategies in Social Interaction*, Cambridge University Press, Cambridge

Duncan, S. and G. Niederehe (1974) 'On Signalling that it's Your Turn to Speak', *Journal of Experimental Social Psychology, 10*, 234-47

Goffman, E. (1976) 'Replies and Responses', *Language in Society, 5*, 257-313

Good, D. (1978) 'On (Doing) Being Hesitant', *Pragmatics Microfiche, 3.2*

—— and B. Butterworth (1978) 'Hesitancy as a Conversational Resource: Some Methodological Implications', unpublished MS, Psychological Laboratory, University of Cambridge, Cambridge

Jefferson, G. (1972) 'Side Sequences', in D. Sudnow (ed.), *Studies in Social Interaction*, Free Press, New York

—— (forthcoming) 'A Technique for Inviting Laughter and its Subsequent Acceptance/Declination', to appear in G. Psathas (ed.), *Everyday Language: Studies in Ethnomethodology*, Irvington, Boston

Katz, J. (1977) *Propositional Structure and Illocutionary Force*, Harvester Press, New York

Lakoff, R. (1973) 'Questionable Answers and Answerable Questions', in B. Kachru *et al.* (eds.) *Issues in Linguistics*, University of Illinois Press, Urbana

Owen, M.L. (1979) 'Units of Natural Conversation', *Pragmatics Microfiche, 3.5*

—— (1980) 'Remedial Interchanges: A Study of Language Use in Social Interaction', unpublished PhD thesis, University of Cambridge, Cambridge

Pomerantz, A. (1975) 'Second Assessments: A Study of Some Features of Agreements/Disagreements', unpublished PhD thesis, University of California, Irvine

—— (1977) 'Agreeing and Disagreeing with Assessments: Some Features of Preferred/Dispreferred Turn Shapes', unpublished MS

Sacks, H., E. Schegloff and G. Jefferson (1974) 'A Simplest Systematics for the Organisation of Turn-Taking for Conversation', *Language, 50, 4*, 696-735

Schegloff, E. (1972) 'Sequencing in Conversational Openings', in Gumperz and Hymes (eds.) *Directions in Sociolinguistics*, Holt, Rinehart, New York. Originally published in *American Anthropologist, 70, 6*, (1968)

—— (1976) 'On Some Questions and Ambiguities in Conversation', *Pragmatics Microfiche, 2.2*

—— and H. Sacks (1974) 'Opening Up Closings', in R. Turner (ed.) *Ethnomethodology*, Penguin, Harmondsworth. Originally published in *Semiotica, 8* (1973) 289-327

Weiser, A. (1974) 'Deliberate Ambiguity', in *Papers of the Tenth Regional Meeting of the Chicago Linguistics Society*, 723-31

Wootton, A.J. (1978) 'The Management of Grantings and Rejections by Parents in Request Sequences', MS, Department of Sociology, University of York

# 6 THEMATISATION IN LUO

## Chet A. Creider

## Introduction

This paper is divided into two parts. In the first, arguments are presented in support of the thesis that in Luo[1] the initial constituent in a sentence is marked for the relational function *theme*,[2] the remainder of the sentence then constituting the *rheme*. We shall see that several independent syntactic processes have as their function the production of a particular highly constrained type of derived constituent structure.

In the second part we look at the notion of thematisation and its relevance to the problem of explanation in syntax. In brief it is argued that thematisation is a process which can best be understood in terms of the interactional setting. Generalising from this it is suggested that the explanation of a natural syntactic process must not only make reference to that which is cognitively natural (Keenan 1972) and perceptually feasible (Bever and Langendoen 1972), but must also include considerations of interactional motivation. That is, the set of natural syntactic processes found in languages must in part be regarded as due to constraints which stem from the organisation of conversational interaction.

## 1. Theme Processes

### 1.1 The Basic Rule of Thematisation

Luo is an SVO language, but like English it has a rule which fronts almost any NP. This rule may be formulated in the same manner as Ross's Topicalisation transformation in English (Ross 1967). That is, a sentence-internal NP is moved leftward and Chomsky-adjoined to the highest S in the sentence. For example, the rule of Thematisation will derive (2) below from (1):

(1) I can't tell you the story
   **an ɔk aɲal pimoni sɩga·na**
   I neg I-able to-tell-you story
(2) the story I can't tell you
   **sɩgana an ɔk aɲal pimoni**
   story I neg I-able to-tell-you

As (3) indicates, Thematisation is unbounded:

(3)   these visitors, I heard that Onyango said (they) are coming
      **welogι naawinjo nιɔɲaŋgɔ ɔwacɔ nι bi·ro**
      visitors-these past-I-heard that onyango said that [are] -coming

Note that Thematisation works toward the front only. In this respect it is very different from the processes described by Gruber (1967) in 'Topicalisation in Child Language', where sentences of the form S + Theme as well as Theme + S were produced by Mackie. All S + Theme sentences are starred in Luo.

## 1.2 Left-dislocation

As is to be expected Thematisation is subject to the various constraints on 'chopping' rules formulated by Ross (1967). Thus (5) derived from (4) is ungrammatical:

(4)   you can't tell my story
      **in ɔk ιɲal pimo sιga·nda**
      you neg you-able to-tell story-my
(5)   *me, you can't tell story
      ***an ɔk ιnal pimo sιga·nd-**
      me neg you-able to-tell story

However, in these situations the related 'copying' rule of Left-dislocation thematises with a grammatical result:

(6)   me, you can't tell my story
      **an ɔk ιɲal pimo sιga·nda**
      me neg you-able to-tell story-my

In further support of our initial thesis, note that just as Thematisation has no backing counterpart, there is no rule of Right-dislocation in Luo. (8) below is derived from (7) by Left-dislocation, but (9) and (10), with Right-dislocation, are ungrammatical.[3]

(7)   the teacher talked to the students about the game
      **japuoŋj noolosonι jopouɲre kuom tu·go**
      teacher past-talked-them students about game
(8)   the students, the teacher talked to them about the game
      **jopuoɲre japuoŋj noolosonιgi kuom tu·go**

students teacher past-talked-them about game
(9)     he talked to the students about the game, the teacher
        *ɛn noolosonɩ jopuoɲre kuom tugo japuo·ɲj
        he past-talked-them students about game teacher
(10)    the teacher talked to them about the game, the students
        *japuoɲj noolosonɩgɩ kuom tugo jopuo·ɲjre
        teacher past-talked-them about game students

## 1.3 Verb Copying

Thematisation and left-dislocation together make it possible to front most of the noun phrases in a sentence. Neither rule applies to constituents of the category Verb. Furthermore, as the examples above show, Luo has a subject-copying rule. Fronting this complex constituent would not amount to thematising Verb alone. In fact it is the verb alone which is fronted in infinitival form by a copying rule. This rule will derive (12) below from (11).

(11)    I said it is necessary that I come
        an naawacɔ nɩ onego abi
        I past-I-said that it-is-necessary I-come
(12)    saying, I said it is necessary that I come
        wacɔ naawacɔ nɩ onego abi
        saying past-I-said that it-is-necessary I-come

## 1.4 Question Words

The interrogative pronouns, ŋa 'who' and aŋɔ 'what', are restricted to post-verbal position when functioning as objects in simplex sentences as shown in (13)–(14):

(13a) who is the doctor?
        ajwɔga ɛn ŋa?                    [*ŋa ɛn ajwɔ·ga?]
        doctor is who                    who is doctor
(13b) what is meat?
        riŋo ɛn aŋɔ?                     [*aŋɔ ɛn ri·ŋo?]
        meat is what                     what is meat
(14a) who do you see?
        ɩnɛnɔ aŋɔ?                       [*aŋɔ ɩnɛ·nɔ?]
        you-see who                      who you-see
(14b) what do you see?
        ɩnɛnɔ aŋɔ?                       [*aŋɔ ɩnɛ·nɔ?]
        you-see what                     what you-see

It is clear, however, that interrogative pronouns are 'precisely what is being talked about' (Halliday 1967:212), and hence are naturally thematic. And indeed, these question words may be fronted by Relativisation as shown in sentences (15-16):

(15a) who is the doctor?
    **ŋa ma ajwɔ·ga?**
    who rel doctor
(15b) what is meat?
    **aŋɔ ma ri·no**
    what rel meat
(16a) who do you see?
    **ŋa ma ɪnɛ·nɔ?**
    who rel you-see
(16b) what do you see?
    **aŋɔ ma ɪnɛ·nɔ?**
    what rel you-see

**ŋa** and **aŋo** may not appear as subjects in simplex sentences in Luo as shown in (17).[4]

(17a) who is coming?
    *****ŋa bi·ro?**
    who is-coming
(17b) what is coming?
    *****aŋɔ bi·ro?**
    what is-coming

Hence only the relativised versions shown in (18) are found.

(18a) who is coming?
    **ŋa ma bi·ro?**
    who rel coming
(18b) what is coming?
    **aŋɔ ma bi·ro?**
    what rel coming

Relativisation also produces other fronted question words, as shown in (19) and (20):

(19)  where were they eating?

nee giciemo ka·ɲɛ?      [\*kaɲɛ nee gicie·mo?]
past they-eating where     where past they-eating

(20) where were they eating?
kaɲ ma nee giciemee
where rel past they-eating-at

Each of (16) and (18) may optionally appear with the third person pronoun copula ɛn in initial position suggesting that a full account of the derivation of these sentences will involve a consideration of clefting as well as relative clause formation. For our purposes here it suffices to establish that means exist for the fronting of question words. The fronted versions occur with overwhelming frequency in actual usage and in addition are the versions spontaneously produced by informants in translation exercises.

It is by now clear that initial position in the derived Luo sentence is not in any sense 'reserved' for the grammatical subject. It is not the case that word order is not relatively fixed in Luo, however, as post-verbal positions are in general filled only by constituents in certain functional relationships in the sentence. For example, (21) is unacceptable because it is interpreted as giving the boy's chickens to the food. The order indirect object + direct object is necessary (22).

(21) we gave food to the boy's chickens
\*wamιyɔ ciemo guend rawɛ·ra
we-gave food chickens-of boy

(22) we gave the boy's chickens food
wamιyɔ guend rawɛra cie·mo
we-gave chickens-of boy food

The finite verb in Luo generally has phonologically reduced forms of self-standing pronouns prefixed to the verb stem as subject-markers. Sentences which have such verbal forms in initial position occur frequently in natural conversation. Examination of these suggests that they occur in conjunction with themes previously stated and that the theme of the previous sentence is understood to be carried over into the next sentence. No other element in such sentences could reasonably be called thematic. Hence what is superficially an exception to the generalisation that initial position is thematic is in fact not an exception at all. Examples of sentences with unmarked theme (or alternatively, with anaphoric themes incorporated into the verb in surface structure) are given in (23) and (24).[5]

(23) A: the people that come from Koyieng' call with cattle outside.
they are coming and returning to our land here.
B: they are returning.
A: **jɔ ma aa koyien rawɔ gι ðok ɔ·kɔ**
people who come-from koyieng' call with cattle outside
**(gi) biro giduogo thurwa ka/**
they-come they-return land-our here
B: **(gi) duo·go/**
they are returning.
(24) A: but we, we built up to Kang'o the place of Kitoto and up to
Nyabera and we covered all of Dunga.
A: **tɔ wan wagedo ɲaka kaŋo ka kito·to/**
but we we-built up-to Kang'o place-of Kitoto
**tɔ ɲaka ɲabɛ·ra/ tɔ (wa) tieko doŋga tɛ/**
and up-to Nyabera and we-finished Dunga all

In sum, we have six kinds of arguments in support of viewing initial
position as thematic in Luo. First is the existence of a number of syntactic
processes such as Thematisation, Left-dislocation and Verb ·Copying,
which move sentence constituents to the extreme left position in the
sentence. Second is the conspicuous absence of analogous movements
to the other end of the sentence. Thirdly we note that Thematisation
and Left-dislocation are related in an important way: Left-dislocation
applies in those situations where Thematisation cannot apply and
together with Verb Copying effectively increases the resources of the
language for thematising sentence constituents. Fourthly, we note that
inherently thematic items such as interrogatives regularly occur initially.
Fifthly, we note the relative rigidity of word order outside of initial
position. Finally sentences without themes in initial position turn
out to presuppose the theme of the previous sentence.[6]

## 2. The Significance of Thematisation

### 2.1 Why thematisation?

Given that a language has a theme function and that it is realised by
the placing of the thematic material in sentence-initial position, two
questions arise. Why should languages have theme processes and why
should they involve fronting? I suggest that the most sensible explan-
ations for these problems exploit the fact that language is sensitive
to the exigencies of the contexts in which it is used. For Luo, at
least until recently, the fundamental context has been conversational

interaction, and it is there that we must look for an understanding of the nature of thematisation.

The organisation of conversation has been the subject of intensive investigation in recent years by Sacks and Schegloff and their students and colleagues. It has been shown that much of the orderliness of conversation centres around the system of turn-taking (Sacks, Schegloff and Jefferson 1974) and further that this system is a local one (i.e. one which proceeds roughly turn by turn).

The relevance of this to theme is the following. Theme is the initial declaration by a speaker of what his utterance is about. In so declaring the speaker exercises his initial option to define the terms of turn-taking, i.e. to set up the frame in which change of turn takes place.

The importance of having the theme at the beginning for turn-taking is argued at length in Sacks (1972a) where it is suggested that, for example, the reason question words are normally in initial position in English has to do with the fact that question words are devices by which current speakers select next speakers other than themselves. The initial question word lets the listener know that he is being selected as next speaker and hence that he must listen to what is being said.

Themes which do not select the next speaker also have functions which are relevant to turn-taking: by telling the listener what the speaker's talk is about these themes define a permissible 'floor' for the speaker — they legitimate his right to continue uninterrupted. In fact, in Luo, one finds that interruptions do not just occur in the place that they might be expected to occur if their occurrence was due to chance alone. They often occur where a speaker's utterance is at variance with his announced theme. The following examples (25) and (26) illustrate this kind of interruption. The conversations are between two Luo elders.[7]

(25) B: but our people that went to Kowak yonder, say to Kanyidoto
        (or) if you go to the lands over that way you find, uh . . .
        what clan or section Kajulu (location of speakers) (//)?

    A: they are returning. the people that come from Koyieng'
        call with cattle outside.

    B: tɔ . . . yawa ma nɔɔðhɩ lɔka kɔwak i . . . kɩa
        but people-our that past-went yonder Kowak uh say
        kaɲido·to k[a] ɩðɩ ɛ pɩɲjɛ ma lɔka kɔnɔ ɩnwaɲɔ
        Kanyidoto if you-go to lands rel yonder say-that you-find
        i . . . kaju·lu/ kɩa ðɔɔt ma·nɛ/ kɩa/ ki-kɔn ma·nɛ/ (//)
        uh Kajulu say clan what say section what

A: giduo·go/ jɔma aa koyieŋ rawɔ gi ðok ɔ·kɔ
they-return people who come-from Koyieng' call with cattle
outside

(26) A: Uyoma then ends at the lake of the people that– . . .

B: Uyoma // ends at

A: the language of these Mwa

B: it ends (at) ends (at) ends (at) Mirunda.

A: ɷyɔma tɔ ɔðι ogikɛ nam mar jɔma . . . jɔka ɔk
Uyoma then it-goes it-ends at lake of people-that people-
those neg

ðɔgι nɛɛ calɔ . . . //
language-their past like

B: ɷyɔm[a] // ogik
Uyoma ends (at)

A: ðɔ mwagι
language of Mwa-these

B: ogik ogik ogik mιrɷ·nda
ends (at) ends (at) ends (at) Mirunda

In (25) B's announced theme is 'our people', but he strays to a
consideration of the place the people had gone to. The interruption
by A contains only theme-relevant content. In (26) the announced
theme is *Uyoma*, a location. A wanders from the theme, B comes
in on a vocalised hesitation pause by A with a reassertion of the theme,
and is interrupted by A who, however, does not complete his utterance.
B terminates the sequence with reference to the understood theme
(*Uyoma*).

The provision of a floor for a turn is related to a second function of
thematisation: the provision of interpretive context or the setting up
of a frame in terms of which understanding of what the speaker says is
to take place. While the function theme is, I believe, distinct from the
given/new information function, it is not unrelated: while theme is not
'given' it is none the less the most important syntactic device in terms
of which the speaker renders his speech 'understandable'. It is that
which the subsequent (in the stream of speech) is to be seen in terms
of (see Sacks 1972b). Clearly it is desirable that such an item be placed
in a fixed position, and of the two most readily available fixed positions,
initial and final, final position has the disadvantage that it may be
presumed that far more often than not a sudden reinterpretation of
the content of the previous utterance would be occasioned by the
announcement of the (final) theme.

## 2.2 The Relevance of Thematisation to the Problem of Explanation in Syntax

I would like to suggest that it is appropriate, particularly in the area of syntax, to return to a consideration of the meaning of features of languages in terms of their communicational functions. We now have, at the very least, fairly full descriptive theories for talking about syntactic phenomena and conversational (and other communicational) phenomena. I think there is a lot of unexplored explanatory potential to be disclosed by viewing the facts we have seen in these phenomena side by side.

In this paper I have tried to show that placement of thematic material in initial position in a sentence is well-motivated in terms of a number of considerations of conversational organisation and that a number of distinct syntactic processes in Luo seem to have been formulated to accomplish just this initial placement.

Luo is a language which until recently was not written. Whatever syntactic processes it has were developed in a context of usage which was, simply, conversational interaction. In this sense conversation may be seen as the environment in which Luo (and most other languages) exist, and, to continue with the biological metaphor, conversation is the environment for which language features are selected.

There are, to my knowledge, only two proposals which have been advanced for the general explanation of the form of syntactic processes in languages. The first is the postulated relationship between the logical structure of utterances and their surface syntactic structure. This approach is argued persuasively in Keenan (1972) and also in Bartsch and Vennemann (1973). Second is the relationship between perceptual processing and syntactic process (Bever and Langendoen 1972). The explanatory efficiency of perceptual constraints for syntax is elegantly demonstrated in Kuno (1974). The explanatory notion I am advancing here is to be understood as additional to these other two. This paper cannot be regarded as in any way definitively establishing the explanatory relevance of conversational organisation for syntax, but it does render such a consideration plausible, and I hope it will prove stimulating to other linguists who like myself feel that recent work in the sequential organisation of conversation (e.g. Sacks *et al.* 1974) is potentially of great importance for an adequate understanding of language.[8]

## Notes

1. Luo is a Nilotic language (Nilo-Saharan family) with some two million

speakers located principally in Kenya but also in Tanzania and Uganda. Although published description of Luo is scarce (see Tucker and Bryan 1966), a full reference grammar of the language has been prepared by A.N. Tucker and will appear shortly. I would like to thank Professor Tucker for his kind help at many points in my work, and also to thank Mr S.J. Ong'or for an immense amount of assistance extending now over a period of several years. Neither are responsible in any way for any errors contained in this work. Luo is a tone language, but tonal diacritics have been omitted for convenience's sake here. Anyone wishing to may obtain a tone-marked set of the Luo utterances used here from me. This work is in part based on a study of video-taped conversations recorded in Kenya in 1971-2. For permission to engage in this research I am indebted to the Kenya Government and for financial assistance to NIH (Grant No. GM 01164) and NSF (Grant No. 2790) administered by the University of Minnesota.

2. The term theme is used in preference to the more familiar term topic for the following reasons:

(1) Theme is the earlier term, preceding topic by several decades (Vachek 1966:18).

(2) Topic is often conflated with focus and the distinction between 'given' and 'new' information. This conflation is also part of the Prague School definition of theme, but in the most recent extensive treatment of thematisation in English, that of Halliday (1967-8), theme is defined independently of the given/new distinction.

(3) I prefer to reserve 'topic' for its traditional usage in the description of the content of discourse (i.e. where the application of the term is not restricted to processes which have been fully grammaticised). It is also in this traditional sense that Sacks and his colleagues use the term.

3. (10) has a reading, 'the teacher talked to them about the students' playing', where –gi 'them' is not necessarily co-referential with jopuo·njre 'the students'.

4. (17a), which is ungrammatical, must not be confused with ŋaa bi·ro 'who is coming' (<ŋa ma bi·ro, cf. 18a).

5. Tape Sources: Sentence (23) is excerpted from VT 20-1; 42-3. Sentence (24) from VT 20-1; 18. Special notation used in this and subsequent utterances: / tone group boundary, . . . filled hesitation, () unclear portion of conversation, // point at which overlap (given in following line) begins.

6. English is another SVO language for which it has been extensively argued that initial position in the sentence is thematic (Mathesius 1928, Vachek 1966, Halliday 1967). There are, however, differences between the means used in English to thematise sentence elements and those used in Luo. Although at the moment any kind of comparative functional syntax is beyond our (at least my) grasp, I discuss English thematisation briefly below in order to illustrate the kinds of facts which such a comparative theory must be able to deal with. The discussion is particularly indebted to Halliday's analyses (1967, 1973).

In English there is a fundamental bifurcation of means used for thematisation which is not found in Luo. The two types of themes found, called unmarked and marked by Halliday, are quite simply characterised (for declarative sentences) as themes with (surface) subject in initial position and themes with some other element in initial position. Marked themes are derived with basically the same means in English as in Luo (e.g. 'This sentence I can't stand'), but there is an important difference in that many marked themes are undeniably unusual in English and the marked word order is distinguished intonationally. This is not at all true in Luo where sentences derived via Thematisation and Left-dislocation are perfectly ordinary (e.g. constituents fronted by Thematisation and Left-dislocation are not marked by an obligatory 'comma' pause in Luo). It has been argued by both Prague School linguists and by Halliday that because English word order is relatively fixed it has been necessary for English to utilise and develop syntactic processes which in effect make surface subjects out of elements which at a deeper stage in derivation are not subjects. The example most often cited is Passivisation. Another example is Raising (e.g. 'That roadrunner seems to be laughing.').

7. (25) is excerpted from VT 20-1, 41-2. (26) is excerpted from VT 26-1; 121-4.

8. A recent study by Langacker (1974) proposes what might appear to be an alternative functional explanation for the processes described here: fronting (and raising) rules 'serve to make the objective content of sentences more prominent' (1974:650). (By 'objective content' Langacker indicates that he means 'propositional content' i.e. the content of the proposition with respect to which an assertion, question, etc., is made). Note first that Langacker is offering only a descriptive generalisation and not an explanation for these syntactic processes. Secondly, note that the generalisation is misleading: fronting and raising rules do not typically render the entire propositional content of sentences more prominent. Rather they typically front or raise NPs, and furthermore these prepositioned items typically are thematic. The thematisation-as-conversationally-motivated perspective offered here is both more accurate descriptively and has explanatory potential.

# References

Bartsch, R. and T. Vennemann (1972) *Semantic Structures*, Athenaum Verlag, Frankfurt

Bever, T.G. and D.T. Langendoen (1972) 'The interaction of speech perception and grammatical structure in the evolution of language', in R.P. Stockwell and R.K.S. Macaulay (eds.) *Linguistic Change and Generative Theory*, Indiana University Press, Bloomington

Gruber, J.S. (1967) 'Topicalization in child language', *Foundations of Language, 3*, 37-65

Halliday, M.A.K. (1967) 'Notes on transitivity and theme in English. Part 2', *Journal of Linguistics, 3*, 199-244

–– (1973) *Explorations in the Functions of Language*, Edward Arnold, London

Keenan, E.L. (1972) 'On semantically based grammar', *Linguistic Inquiry, 3*, 413-61

Kuno, S. (1974) 'The position of relative clauses and conjunctions', *Linguistic Inquiry, 5*, 117-36

Langacker, R.W. (1974) 'Movement rules in functional perspective', *Language, 50*, 630-64

Mathesius, V. (1928) 'On linguistic characterology with illustrations from modern English', *Actes du Premier Congrès International de Linguistes à La Haye*, pp. 56-66. Reprinted in Vachek (ed.) (1964), pp. 59-67

Ross, J.R. (1967) 'Constraints on Variables in Syntax', M.I.T. dissertation

Sacks, H. (1972a) 'Lectures on Adjacency Pairs', Department of Sociology, University of California at Irvine, Irvine

–– (1972b) 'On some puns: with some intimations', in R.W. Shuy (ed.) *Report of the Twenty-third Annual Round Table Meeting on Linguistics and Language Studies*, Georgetown University Press, Washington, pp. 135-44

–– E.A. Schegloff and G. Jefferson (1974) 'A simplest systematics for the organization of turn-taking for conversation', *Language, 50*, 696-735

Tucker, A.N. and M.A. Bryan (1966) *Linguistic Analyses: The non-Bantu Languages of North-Eastern Africa*, Oxford University Press for International African Institute, Oxford

Vachek, J. (ed.) (1964) *A Prague School Reader in Linguistics,* Indiana University Press, Bloomington
−− (ed.) (1966) *The Linguistic School of Prague*, Indiana University Press, Bloomington

# 7 THE CONCEPT OF 'RELEVANCE' IN CONVERSATIONAL ANALYSIS

Paul Werth

## 1. Ethnomethodology and Pragmatics

I want first to discuss briefly two very different approaches to the analysis of conversational interaction, before introducing a third. These are: first, that of the ethnomethodologists, particularly Sacks, Schegloff and Jefferson 1974; and secondly, that of the pragmatists, especially Grice 1975. The ethnomethodologists are primarily concerned with the tacit rules which regulate the taking-up by speakers of the running topic, and hence the change-over from one speaker to another. The points at which change-overs occur are called places of **transition-relevance**, which take place at 'possible completion points' (p. 707), and 'these turn out to be "possible completion points" of sentences, clauses, phrases, and one-word constructions, and multiples thereof' (p. 721), i.e. in linguistic terms, syntactic constituents. However, they maintain (p. 725, fn. 38) that it is the turn-taking system itself which determines that, for instance, an answer should follow a question, and not any inherent linguistic feature of the utterance. (We shall challenge this claim presently.) Their account of conversational interchange, in other words, predicts that the socio-psychological system of turn-taking overrides various possible linguistic indicators to the contrary. (There appear to be problems with this prediction, though: how can we account for rhetorical questions, or commands and requests in the form of questions, for example?) Syntactic constituents, according to them, do not *determine* places of transition-relevance; rather, they merely provide *potential loci* for places of transition-relevance. We have still, therefore, to decide what actually is meant by the notion of 'relevance': could it be a semantic/pragmatic notion? Something of this kind seems likely, for towards the end of their paper, Sacks, Schegloff and Jefferson remark that the whole system

> can be brought under the jurisdiction of perhaps the most general principle which particularizes conversational interactions, that of **recipient design**. By 'recipient design' we refer to a multitude of respects in which the talk by a party in a conversation is constructed

> or designed in ways which display an orientation and sensitivity to
> the particular other(s) who are the co-participants . . . with regard
> to word-selection, topic selection, admissibility and ordering of
> sequences, options and obligations for starting and terminating
> conversations etc. (p. 727)

They also relate recipient design to context-sensitivity (though not,
presumably, in its formal sense). It would seem then, that the term
'relevance' has for them something like its ordinary meaning of 'semantic
appropriateness'. Furthermore, they claim for the turn-taking system
that it places an obligation on an intending speaker to listen carefully
to the turn before; this is not only to monitor it in case he is selected as
next speaker, but also so that his contribution might be appropriately
fashioned to what precedes it (e.g. greeting-response, question-answer,
insult-riposte, and so on). This clearly requires that he pays attention
to the *meaning* of what goes before: I shall presently suggest what the
machinery of this process might be.

Grice too makes crucial use of the notion of appropriateness or
relevance. His 'Co-operative Principle' of conversation (1975:45–6) has
four 'maxims', namely Quality, Quantity, Manner and Relation. The
last of these, succinctly stated, is 'Be relevant'; in other words, participants in a conversation actively assume each other's co-operation: it is
assumed that contributions are intended to follow on from verbal
and/or situational context. Grice in fact admits to finding a precise
characterisation of relevance 'extremely difficult', and has little to offer
by way of definition, except the following: 'I expect a partner's contribution to be appropriate to immediate needs at each stage of the
transaction' (1975:47), which merely substitutes for the word 'relevant',
its virtual synonym 'appropriate'. If a speaker observes the Co-operative
Principle (CP) and its maxims, then the hearer is able to perceive a
clear relationship between the latest contribution and what has gone
before. If this relationship is not an obvious one, then Grice's notion of
**conversational implicature** comes into play. This allows the listener to
continue to assume relevance, but forces him to search for it via connections which are more obscure, e.g. through irony, insinuation,
sarcasm or innuendo. Relevance is assumed, then, even if all appearances
are against it. Again, underlying this constant search for relevance in
conversation is a continuous process of semantic monitoring: in order
to determine whether B is relevant to A, one must have access to the
meaning of both A and B:

To work out that a particular conversational implicature is present, the hearer will rely on ... the fact (or supposed fact) that all relevant items falling under [(1) conventional meaning of terms + identity of references; (2) CP and maxims; (3) context; (4) background knowledge] are available to both participants and both participants know or assume this to be the case (1975:50)

These two schools of thought seem to me to be in no way conflicting. Indeed, the concept of 'co-operation' seems to have a great deal in common with the concept of 'recipient design'. But whereas the ethnomethodologists are concerned with when and why A's turn gives way to B's turn, Grice is concerned with how B's contribution is related to A's contribution. Both, as I've tried to show, make crucial use of the semantic/pragmatic notion of relevance, which requires a comparison between preceding and following in terms of semantic structure and implications. Neither the ethnomethodologists nor Grice say anything about this crucial factor in conversational interchange, so I will presently attempt to fill the gap.

However, since 1967, when Grice's ideas on conversational logic were first made public, some scholars have taken up the concept of relevance and attempted to give it a more rigorous treatment within Grice's framework. A crucial notion has been that of the **pragmatic presupposition**, the set of which informing a particular interchange is the **common ground**. Both of these rely essentially upon the notion of context; compare for example, Karttunen 1977:

Context X satisfies-the-presuppositions-of S just in case the presuppositions of each of the constituent sentences in S are satisfied by the corresponding local context. (1977:153)

... a conversational context, a set of logical forms, specifies what can be taken for granted in making the next speech act. What this common set of background assumptions contains depends on what has been said previously and other aspects of the communicative situation ... At each step along the way ... the current context satisfies the presuppositions of the next sentence that in turn increments it to a new context (1977:155-6)

In a later paper, Karttunen and Peters (1979) are a little more explicit about these 'other aspects of the communicative system', and also about the process of 'incrementation':

Imagine a group of people engaged in an exchange of talk. At each point in their conversation there is a set of propositions that any participant is rationally justified in taking for granted, for example, by virtue of what has been said in the conversation up to that point, what all the participants are in a position to perceive as true, whatever else they mutually know, assume, and so on. This set of propositions is what we call the common ground . . . When a participant says something, thereby advancing the conversation to a new point, the new set of common presumptions reflects the change from the preceding set in terms of adjunction, replacement, or excision of propositions. (1979:13-14)

Finally, Wilson and Sperber (1978 and this volume), dealing directly with the notion of relevance, see it as a relationship between the current proposition and this common ground: '. . . relevance is a relation between the proposition expressed by an utterance, on the one hand, and the set of propositions in the hearer's accessible memory on the other' (p. 169). In another paper (Wilson and Sperber 1979), they describe the nature of this relationship in more detail. Given the current proposition P, many other propositions are related to P either because they entail P or because they are entailed by P; (there are also, of course, even more propositions which hold neither relation to P). Wilson and Sperber show that the P-entailed or P-entailing propositions can be ordered logically, and that the higher-ordered an entailment is, the more relevant to P it is. However, this ordering, though internally logical, is externally (pragmatically) determined by the context of utterance, i.e. the common ground: in particular, which of P's entailments are relevant to the exchange depends on which of them occur in the set of propositions in the common ground, i.e. which of them has been accepted by the interlocutors (having been asserted or entailed previously) as part of the common pool of shared information.

In the next section, I shall describe a model of conversation within which the relevance of an utterance is indicated. However, before summarising the view of contextual dependency which we have arrived at, I must first comment on some criticisms of this view advanced by Gerald Gazdar (1979:105-7): 'The first is that utterances which have a presupposition that clashes with the context are not *infelicitous* . . . etc.; they simply lose the presupposition.' Thus, a sentence like

1. So John doesn't regret killing his father

which *in isolation* presupposes 'John killed his father', may well not presuppose this in an actual context (e.g. where the speaker has just been convinced that John did not kill his father, and therefore that some previous assertion that John regretted this act could not possibly be the case). The first point here is that while we may speak of a sentence, or even a proposition, bearing a presupposition, it does not seem to make sense to say that *utterances* do so. An utterance, as Gazdar reasonably defines it (e.g. p. 4), is a sentence-context pair. Thus if presuppositions are correctly regarded as propositions occurring in the context (i.e. the common ground), they are *explicitly* present in an utterance, but only implicitly present in a sentence. They may be observed in a discourse-grammar, but remain mysterious in a sentence-grammar. The second point is that, as an utterance, (1) may have different emphatic structures (a notion I will describe presently) depending on the different contexts it may be embedded in. The written form (1), that is to say, does not evince any properties of contextualisation: as the representation of an *utterance*, therefore, it is deficient. A more utterance-explicit form, then, might look like one of:

2. (a) So [John] DOESN'T [regret] [killing] his [father][1]
   (b) So [John] doesn't REGRET [killing] his [father]

to mention just two possibilities. (b) has the presupposition (or is, rather, based on the common-ground proposition) that John killed his father, and asserts the incorrectness of some previous proposition that he regrets the act. (a) is interesting, because even in this more explicit form it is still ambiguous between (i) a denial that John *regrets* killing his father, preserving the presupposition in question (i.e. similar to (2b)); and (ii) a denial of the whole sentence, cancelling the presupposition in question. However, this ambiguity is an artefact of the contextless state of (2a): as Gerald Gazdar stipulates, given an appropriate context (i.e. one in which the proposition that John killed his father is either accepted or rejected), sentence (2a) (or its less explicit counterpart (1)) will bear the 'presupposition' or not. His further point, 'that (1) presupposes [the presupposition in question] *unless* the context indicates the contrary', lacks any substance, of course, in an approach which always requires the context to be specified.

Gazdar's second main objection to the contextual account is that it requires an actual contextually-explicit entailment for each 'presupposition', including those found in context-initial utterances (for which, presumably, no pool of contextual information has yet had the chance to come into existence). (The standard sentence-grammar account, conversely, must regard *every* sentence as context-initial, and cannot accommodate any functions which are sensitive to contextual information.) But consider such an account of contextual incrementation as the Karttunen-Peters one above. If we regard the process of incrementation as the result of speaker and hearer **negotiating** for the acceptance of information (as is always claimed in ethnomethodological accounts), then there is no reason to assume that a given proposition is either in the common ground or not; there is a third state possible, namely 'pending', in which an assertion or any entailments associated with it have been uttered — are being negotiated — but have not yet been entered into the common ground. (McCawley 1979 recognises **temporary incrementation** as a device in the interpretation of both assertions containing definite descriptions and also the consequent clauses of conditionals. Gazdar's own solution amounts to this too: he requires P to be *consistent with* the common ground, rather than the stronger 'be entailed by', and has a category of **potential presuppositions** which may be cancelled by contradictory elements in the context.)

## 2. Towards a Model of Conversation

The model of conversation which all of these accounts seem to suggest, therefore, is a co-operative venture in which the participants seek to increment the commonly-accepted set of propositions by contributing further propositions which are relevant to it. The current speaker, that is to say, puts up some propositional information as a relevant contribution; the listener either accepts it (with a 'back channel feature', signifying agreement, or at least compliance) or rejects it (with a contrastive feature of contradiction, plus some justification for this in the form of propositional information); the listener may go on to add a further contribution, subject to the same constraints of relevance. So, making the simplifying assumption that conversation is straightforward dialogue, i.e. an alternation between two speakers, each one processing his own contributions and those of the other, constantly monitoring them for relevance, we can illustrate the whole process by Figure 7.1. In this figure, A, B, C and D are alternate speakers. Each speaker initiates a 'message' of propositional information which he has selected, guided by the set of common assumptions already present, and which he regards as relevant (or may be assumed by the hearer to do so).

**Figure 7.1: A Model of the Conversational Process**

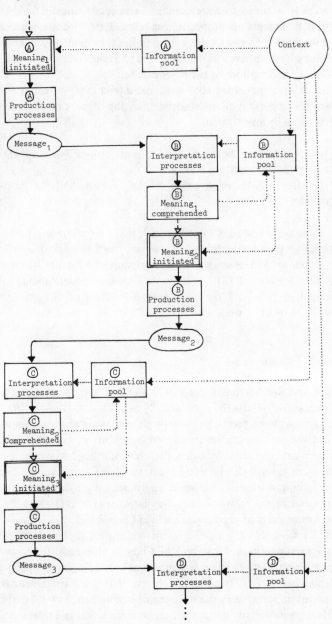

The hearer, guided by the CP, acts on the assumption that the current contribution is intended to be relevant and assesses it critically for that property. If he accepts the proposition as relevant, its semantic content is added to, deleted from or otherwise modifies the cumulative pool of information which we have variously referred to as the common ground, set of common assumptions or the pragmatic set.

Having set up a model for conversational interchange, we can more clearly see the important questions concerning the concept of relevance which remain to be investigated:

(i)  the relationship between the current proposition and the contextual information pool; and

(ii) the effect of this relationship on the expression of the proposition.

Both of these are presumably matters which are of more concern to the current speaker than to the listener. However, when faced with a well-formed utterance, and assuming it to be relevant, the listener will use the linguistic features of (ii), together with his own understanding of the information pool and the propositional content of the current contribution in order to work out (i).

## 3. Linguistic Features

As Wilson and Sperber point out (1979:304-5): 'a speaker may use linguistic means to indicate the pragmatically most important entailments of his utterance. More precisely, he may place them in the foreground of the ordered set of entailments carried by his utterance.' This is in line with a recent comment by Grice, slightly modifying his conception of implicature as completely non-formal: 'a slight extension to the maxim enjoining relevance, making it apply not only to what is said, but to features of the means used for saying what is said' (1978:122). It is also in the spirit of suggestions made in Chomsky (1972) based on Jackendoff's work (1972), namely those concerning the concepts of **focus** and **presupposition**. However, the Chomsky-Jackendoff account assumes that (contrastive) stress is a superficial phonological property. Wilson and Sperber (1979) correctly observe that stress assignment is of paramount importance in the ordering of entailments. I shall briefly review their treatment of the interaction between stress and relevance, before suggesting how the assignment of stress and related phenomena actually takes place in connected discourse.

Wilson and Sperber, investigating the possibility that sentences with the same propositional content may nevertheless differ semantically, put forward four claims (pp. 313–15):

(i) Given a sentence such as:
   3. You've eaten all my APPLES,
   with stress (of some kind) as indicated, it is possible mechanically to replace any constituent containing the stressed item (viz: *apples, my apples, all my apples, eaten all my apples*, or *you've eaten all my apples*) with a variable (which we can represent by *something, someone, do something*). Each such expression is a **grammatically specified entailment**, and the first claim is that such entailments are the only ones that can be indicated by purely linguistic means (such as stress).

(ii) It is therefore important that grammatically specified entailments are naturally ordered in terms of the hierarchical ordering of the constituents replaced by variables. The second claim is that the order of entailments in any given case is determined by the stress assignment.

(iii) Assuming variable substitution in (3) of *all my apples*, we obtain:
   4. You've eaten something.
   This is the **background** of sentence (3) having focus on *all my apples*. The **foreground** is then all those propositions in the set of grammatically specified entailments which entail (4), namely:
   5. (a) You've eaten *all of something of mine*
       (b) You've eaten *all of someone's apples*
       (c) You've eaten *some quantity of my apples*
       (d) You've eaten *all of something*
   The third claim is that foreground information less information also contained in the background will determine the relevance of the utterance, i.e. the italicised portions of (5).

(iv) The distinction between normal and contrastive stress affects the scope of variable-substitution: contrastive stress narrows it, e.g. (3) with contrast on *apples* has only (5a) as its background.

This set of entailments, then, is determined and selected by means of the stress assignment of the sentence in question. But as I have already pointed out in section 1, Wilson and Sperber also allow for sentence-entailments which are not grammatically specified in the defined sense: the current proposition will bear a large number of such entailments which may, however, be related usefully to the background, as defined above. They may (a) entail the background, (b) be entailed by it, or (c) bear neither relation to the background. The authors show that (broadly speaking) (a) and (b) may contribute to relevance, but (c) may not, though in some circumstances such entailments may contribute to the incrementation of information. In all these cases, though, there must be 'pragmatic reasons indicating their involvement', i.e. in terms of the model we have put forward, there must exist in the information pool propositions themselves asserting or entailing these entailments. I now want to suggest, though, (in line with Karttunen and Peters 1979 and Wilson and Sperber, this volume) that the contextual control of entailments extends to the grammatically-specified ones no less than the others. In fact, I will claim that the relationships contributing to relevance are mostly contextual and may, furthermore, be handled by the machinery for textual coherence.

## 4. Textual Coherence

Consider the following extract from a radio discussion on Virginia Woolf's *To the Lighthouse*. Speaker A is introducing a new sub-topic, so the links with what has gone before are minimal; however, there is some common ground, notably the novel, its author, salient objects and characters, together with items of common knowledge, particularly concerning Freud. The passage has been marked up to display the categories of **emphasis** which I shall discuss presently. These cannot be arrived at by taking surface considerations (e.g. of stress or intonation) alone, but require a combination of surface factors and semantic/ pragmatic factors. A full justification for this claim may be found in Werth (forthcoming: ch. 2). There are four types of emphasis here: ∅ (unmarked), Focus (italics), Reduction (square brackets), and Contrast (capitals).

5. $A^1$: I [wonder] whether when it was FIRST [published] in *nineteen-twenty-seven* — that was, after all, AFTER *Freud*, wasn't it — the *average* READER *recognised* the *very strong sexual symbolism throughout* the [book] : because, of course, the *lighthouse* is a *phallic* [emblem] , and *James*, the [son] , the [little boy James] , who *wants* so *badly* to *go* to the [lighthouse] and is *frustrated* all the *time*, *explicitly hates* his [father] and *wants* to *stab* him to *death*, which *occurs*

> *both* [early] AND [late] in the [book].
>
> B[1] : But just at the *end*, there's a RECONCILIATION.
>
> A[2] : It's this *Oedipus* [thing], really.
>
> C[1] : The [Lighthouse] DOES [raise] all *sorts* of [questions] about what *exactly* the [symbols] ARE, whether in fact you *invent* your OWN, rather, and *put* them *in*. Certainly *one* of them is the [little boy] who, *now* in ADOLESCENCE, *steps* ON to the [lighthouse] and that is his *coming* to MANHOOD, presumably.
>
> A[3] : Well, *quite, yes.*
>
> B[2] : Isn't it *terrible*, I just don't *see* ANY of these [sexual symbols], I never am *aware* of them. I just don't SEE them, I just don't CARE about these [phallic symbols].
>
> C[2] : I [think] they're *meant* to *operate* on an − *not* on a CONSCIOUS *level.*
>
> B[3] : *Good.*
>
> C[3] : And I don't [think] they're MEANT to be OBTRUSIVE.
>
> B[4] : Well, they're NOT [obtrusive] to ME.

**Focus** (F) marks content occurring for the first time (e.g. *Freud, recognised, hates, invent, terrible*) or revived as though occurring for the first time (e.g. *lighthouse* in A[1]). The conditions under which these revivals occur are presumably open to empirical investigation, but they are probably not entirely linguistic. I shall have nothing more to say about this here. **Reduction** (R) also appears on content-words whose content, however, is predictable in one of three ways:

(i) because it has been repeated (with identical reference if it has such), e.g. [lighthouse] (A[1]), [sexual symbols] (B[2]), [obtrusive] (B[4]);

(ii) virtual repetition (i.e. repetition of content without lexical repetition), e.g. (*symbol(ism)*)∼ [emblem] (A[1]);

(iii) implication (i.e. logical or pragmatic entailment), e.g. (*book*)∼ [published] (A[1]), ([son])∼ [father] (A[1]).

**Contrast** (C) occurs on items bearing some semantic or pragmatic connection with some previous' item, though at the same time a denial, explicit or implicit, of identity, e.g. ([little boy])∼ADOLESCENCE∼ MANHOOD, all of which contain the semantic predicate [MATURE] (+ or −): *little* is [−MAT], *adolescence* contains [∼[−MATV+MAT]], while *manhood* contains [+MAT]. Specifically, the latter two deny [−MAT] in the first, while the last denies the disjunction in the second. Finally, the **unmarked** (∅) items are words which have no history of F marking at all; they are, in fact, function-words (as opposed to content-words) which we may assume are not analysable into semantic predicates (though there are problems of recognition here with, for example, pronouns, prepositions and several other categories: see Werth, forthcoming: ch. 2). I shall return to these briefly.

These categories of emphasis, though distinct, nevertheless interact in a regular and interesting way. Let us look a little more closely at a sentence from (5), (exchange $B^2$):

6. (a) I just don't see any of these sexual symbols

I am going to assume that the proposition underlying (6a) can be represented as a bracketed expression of (variables and) predicates. These show both logical dependency in a complex expression (e.g. that between *not* and *any*) as well as syntactic dependency (as in the relationship between *see* and what follows it), including lexical status. Possible lexical status is shown by a predicate or sequence of predicates flanked by brackets and containing no brackets, viz. '(PRED)', ')PRED(', ')PRED)' or '(PRED('. For simplicity, in the present account, I am assuming that predicates are more or less word size, i.e. though further decomposition may be possible I shall not attempt it unless it is necessary for the analysis. Thus, (6b) represents the (simplified) semantic structure of (6a) — but this is *irrespective of context*.

6. (b) ((I) SEE (NOT-ONE ((SEXUAL) SYMBOL)))

However, *in* context, each predicate may carry a variable communicative value, depending on whether (roughly) it represents new or predictable information. In other words, the communicative value (manifested in its emphasis-marking) is sensitive to the information-flow of the discourse. Thus the actual emphatic structure of (6a) in (5) is:

6. (c) I just don't *see* ANY of these [sexual symbols]

In (6c), *see* is focused, because it is a first mention, [sexual symbols] is reduced, since *sexual symbolism* and [symbols] have occurred previously (in $A^1$ and $C^1$), while (not) ANY is contrastive, since its underlying form NOT-ONE both coheres with, and denies, the number of examples of sexual symbols given by the other speakers:

6. (d) $\exists 3x$ (x is an example of sexual symbolism) →
$\exists x$  (x is an example of sexual symbolism)

The entailment of (6d) ('There is at least one example of sexual symbolism [in the book]') thus coheres with (6a) since there is partial repetition of both semantic structure and reference. However, it is also denied by (6a), since the logical form of the sentence is:

6. (e) $\sim \exists x$ (x is an example of sexual symbolism $\wedge$ I see x)

We may also observe that these different manifestations of emphasis are not entirely separate. In fact, they pattern fairly regularly with the independent distinction between content items (nouns, verbs, adjectives and adverbs, roughly) and function items (more or less the remaining categories, although this is actually an oversimplification). Thus F and R can only occur on content items, while $\emptyset$ occurs only on function items; C, however, can occur on either. To put the situation somewhat the other way round, if a function word is stressed, this is inevitably contrastive. However, as I have already claimed, this is something of an over-simplification, as (i) some function words have semantic content; and (ii) there are restrictions on the occurrence of stress with function words. For example, expletive uses of *it* and *there* and complementiser *that* appear to reject stress (and therefore contrast) entirely. I would claim that of all the classes of function-words these are the *least* semantic, and that their non-occurrence with stress is actually directly related to this fact. I am not going to discuss this any further here, but will take it as evidence that, since what F, R and C have in common is *content*, the correct place to state their relationship in the grammar is in the semantic representation. Before we proceed to state this appropriately, a further point should be noted: R and C share an important property in that both refer back to previous information, i.e. common ground material. Both, that is to say, are **anaphoric**: R positively so (since it requires synonymy of semantic structure or entailments between the reduced item and what we may call its **antecedent**); C negatively (since it requires the negation in the contrastive item of an entailment of its antecedent). We will explore these suggestions in more detail presently.

We can account for the observable facts of the relationship between these varieties of emphasis by postulating a set of ordered rules for emphasis-placement:

7. (a) On each terminal predicate in semantic structure:

$$\ldots \text{Pred} \ldots \rightarrow \ldots \begin{bmatrix} \text{Pred} \\ \text{F} \end{bmatrix} \ldots$$

(b) If within the Universe of Discourse, a predicate is predictable:
$$F \rightarrow R$$

(c) Under the semantic condition for contrast:
$$\begin{Bmatrix} R \\ \emptyset \end{Bmatrix} \rightarrow C$$

(7a) bears a passing resemblance to the Chomsky and Halle Nuclear Stress Rule, though it is stated on semantic predicates. However, they may turn out to be the same. (7b) reduces focused predicates under the condition of positive coherence, which in a somewhat more explicit form is stated as (8a):

8. (a) $\forall x,y, R(x,y) \rightarrow D(x,y) \wedge ((\exists z, (z \varepsilon x) \wedge (z \varepsilon y)) \vee (F(x) \rightarrow F(y)))$
   R – 'reduces' D – 'is in the same Universe of Discourse'
   F – 'any function'

i.e. a reduced item is in the same Universe of Discourse as its antecedent, and either shares some sub-part of its structure with its antecedent (as in cases of repetition or virtual synonymy) or shares an entailment of its antecedent (as in cases of implied connection). (7c) then (re)stresses items for contrast, given compliance with the constraint requiring negative coherence, stated more formally as (8b):

8. (b) $\forall x,y, C(x,y) \rightarrow D(x,y) \wedge \exists z, (z \varepsilon x) \wedge (z \varepsilon y) \wedge \exists w, F(x) \rightarrow F(w)$
   $\wedge F(y) \rightarrow \sim F(w)$
   C – 'contrasts with' D, F – as before

i.e. a contrastive item is in the same Universe of Discourse as its antecedent, and shares some sub-part of its structure with its antecedent. Moreover, there is also some sub-part of its structure which denies an entailment of its antecedent. Part of (8b) is of course identical with part of (8a): this is the section guaranteeing coherence, which in content items confines contrast to pairs with some semantic connection (I except from this **citation-contrast** which is motivated by surface-form – e.g. 'I said [ɔrəl] not [ɑɒrəl]' – and is arguably very different from semantic contrast). However, rule (7c) allows $\emptyset$-marked items to go to C also: $\emptyset$-marked items, it will be remembered, are always function words, but those that can go to C are those with some kind of semantic content. In such cases, possible antecedents vary: prepositions, if contrastive, contrast with other prepositions, but pronouns are likely to contrast with nouns or NPs, and auxiliary verbs might contrast with other auxiliaries or modals, or with the polarity of the antecedent constituent. The disjunction in the input to rule (7c) reflects my current uncertainty as to the precise status of stressed (contrastive) function items, specifically from the point of view of their semantic representation. However, I do not find any more enlightening treatment of such items in other current approaches either.

We can now apply (7) to (6b) to get the actually occurring form (6c):

9. (a)     ((I)   SEE   (NOT-ONE   ((SEXUAL)   SYMBOL)))

| | | | | | |
|---|---|---|---|---|---|
| By (7a): | F | F | F | F | F |
| By (7b): | R | F | R | R | R |
| By (7c): | R | F | C | R | R |
| (b) | | I don't *see* | ANY | [sexual] | [symbols] |

The operation of constraints (8a, b) needs explanation: (7b) operates on (I) because the speaker is always present in the situation; it operates on (SEXUAL) and (SYMBOL) because both occurred previously, i.e. in this case x=y=z; it operates on (NOT-ONE) because, as I have already shown in (6d), at least one sexual symbol has been suggested. Notice that this process must operate structurally as well as semantically, because what is cohesive in (NOT-ONE) is not this predicate by itself, but rather the whole semantic constituent (NOT-ONE((SEXUAL) SYMBOL)). Contrast, (rule (7c)), on the other hand now operates on (NOT-ONE) because it denies (ONE) (=w, in (8b)).

We have established, therefore, that reduction and contrast both display coherence. Does this mean that a focused item does not cohere? Even *prima facie* this seems an unlikely and undesirable requirement, since focused items must, despite their 'newness', nevertheless be relevant to what has gone before. This is the apparent paradox of the notion 'new' in this connection: if an item were really *completely* novel semantically in its context, it might be entirely inappropriate (I except, of course, items which are 'context-forming', e.g. at the beginning of a discourse). So focused items fall into 'lexical chains' linked in semantic field relationships. Consider from passage (5), for example, the chain of F items: *Freud – sexual symbolism – phallic – frustrated – hates – stab – death – Oedipus.* These are somehow linked cognitively in that they all refer to a specific sphere of knowledge, and to some extent are mutually predictive. So, focused items in a discourse also have coherence connections with other items; the question now is, how do they differ from reduced or contrastive items? The answer lies, as we have seen, in the notion of **anaphora**, or textual reference. R and C elements are both anaphoric, F elements are non-anaphoric. Note that anaphora is not the same as coherence. All coherence, as we have seen, involves at least partial similarity of semantic structure, including implications; anaphora, on the other hand, involves **deixis**, i.e. an indexical relationship between elements in the same context. Thus our examples of chains of focused items will be encyclopaedically, i.e. contingently, related; unlike R and C items, however, they are not deictically related, i.e. they cannot be assumed to share identity[2] across a text. They cohere by virtue of their meaning rather than their deixis. (It might be objected that this provides no explanation for reduced NPs with an indefinite article, normally used for first-mention, e.g. 'a *phallic* [emblem]' in $A^1$, where I have argued [emblem] is reduced as a virtual synonym of *symbol(ism)*. But how is it possible to claim a *deictic* relationship between *emblem* and *symbol*, when the existence of an indefinite article suggests first-mention? I would argue that 'a phallic emblem' here in this context has the logical form 'a phallic one of such symbols', i.e. it is an instantiation or member of a previously-mentioned set, and the deixis lies in this relationship. For details of this sort of analysis of determiners, see Werth, 1980.)

So far, I have assumed that predicates are word-size, so that no problems occur in the translation from emphasis-placement to surface emphatic structure. But what happens when, as in a full-fledged analysis would be common, a word decomposed into a complex semantic structure of several predicates contains a non-matching set of emphatic elements? Clearly, something which surfaces as a single lexical item cannot display complex emphatic structure corresponding to the emphases on its complex semantic structure. I propose that emphatic elements are hierarchically ordered, so that

10.  $C > F > R$

Thus any lexical item containing an emphatic complex simplifies it in accordance with (10), e.g.

| 11. | (a) | the little boy who, now in adolescence ... | | | | | | | |
|---|---|---|---|---|---|---|---|---|---|
| | (b) | (LITTLE)(−MATURE +M +H)$_x$ (x NOW (BETWEEN−MAT ∧ +MAT))) | | | | | | | |
| By | (7a) | F | F | F | F | F | F | F | F |
| By | (7b) | R | R | R | R | F | F | R | R |
| | | (cf.A$^1$) | | (−cf.− | A$^1$ −) | | | (−cf.− | A$^1$ −) |
| By | (7c) | R | R | R | R | F | F | R | C |
| | | | | | | | | | (cf.−MA |
| By | (10) | | R | | | | C | | |
| | (c) | the [little] | [boy] | who, *now* in ADOLESCENCE ... | | | | | |

(10) is presumably an output constraint since it must follow lexical insertion, anaphoric marking and emphasis placement, which involve lexico-semantic elements occurring in specific contexts.


## 5. Relevance

At the end of section 2, I suggested that there were two aspects of the notion of relevance in conversation which we needed to investigate:

(i) the relationship between the current proposition and the contextual information pool; and
(ii) the effect of this relationship on the expression of the current proposition.

We can now look at these questions in the light of the ordered entailments view of relevance together with the more detailed view of emphasis-placement set out in the preceding section. With reference to (i), we can see the relationship between the current proposition and the context as a relationship between the meaning + entailments of the current proposition and the propositions in the information pool. This relationship is identical to the notion of **coherence**, as commonly held in European text-linguistics. A succinct statement of coherence viewed as a general textual constraint may be found in Van Dijk 1972:

$$12.\ S \rightarrow \ldots$$
$$X \rightarrow a \quad \bigg/ \left( \begin{matrix} R \equiv \\ R \subset \\ R \ \mathcal{E} \end{matrix} \right) \quad (\delta(\subset S_{\prime}), -)$$
$$Y \rightarrow \beta$$
$$Z \rightarrow \gamma$$

where $a$, $\beta$, $\gamma$ are 'abstract semantic terminal subtrees', at least one of which bears one of the contextual relations (equivalence, inclusion, membership) to $\delta$, which is a subtree of $S_{\prime}$, which precedes S in the discourse. If we take S to be the current proposition plus its entailments, and $S_{\prime}$ to be any proposition in the information pool (rather than a previous sentence in the text), then $a$, $\beta$ and $\gamma$ are 'semantic constituents', i.e. predicates or predicate-variable clusters (which may be, potentially or in fact, word-size), each of which is either equivalent to, included in, or a member of some semantic constituent in the information pool. (We should probably add to these 'contextual relations' $R \supset$, 'implies', and perhaps others.)

(12), or something much like it, governs the ordinary coherence of focused items, we may postulate, and this is one element of the general textual property of **connectivity**; the other main element being the occurrence of connectives (e.g. *and, furthermore, moreover; but, however, nevertheless; so, therefore*). I will say nothing more about these here.

It can, moreover, be argued that (12) has as special cases the two constraints given as (8a) and (8b), namely the positive coherence (reduction) condition, and the negative coherence (contrast) condition. (8a) and (8b) as they stand are *interpretive* conditions, i.e. they allow the hearer to infer contextual connections from the observed fact (or hypothesis) of the presence of R or C. Reverse the initial arrows, though, and the conditions are then production constraints: thus (8a') (the reverse of (8a)) would read 'for any pair of semantic constituents in the same Universe of Discourse, if they have either some element in common or share some implication, then the first reduces the second'. Put like this, (8a') is clearly an instance of (12). Assuming the non-directionality of (12), there is no formal distinction between (8a) and (8a') (though there are, as we have seen, important psychological differences in terms of the *processing* of discourse); by the same token, there is no formal distinction between (8b) and *its* reverse, (8b'), though in this case the processing difference makes (8b') untenable, in my opinion (since I think it is not empirically the case that anything fulfilling the condition for contrast will necessarily receive contrast). One further point about (8) and (12) is that they make no explicit provision for the situational context. I shall take it that the deictic relationship between objects, events etc. in the situation and textual elements in the discourse is semiotically equivalent to the anaphoric relationship between an antecedent and its anaphor in a text, i.e. as Lyons (1977:675) points out, both are deictic. (Some accounts, e.g. Halliday and Hasan (1976) on 'exophora' and Hankamer and Sag (1976) on 'pragmatically controlled anaphora', are prepared to take the similarity as essential identity. But see Huddleston (1978) for a corrective to this viewpoint.) Thus when (12) and (8) stipulate contextual related-ness between elements, I take this to include situational objects as well as textual ones. An immediate practical consequence of this view is that certain textual elements are *automatically* reduced by (7b/8a) as being situationally present (e.g. (I), (YOU)), or conventionally recessive (e.g. (BE), (HAVE), (SOMEONE), (PEOPLE), (THING)). This latter set is characterised by semantic simplicity (presumably, (BE) cannot be analysed further) or generality.

Let us now test these remarks out on some simplified exchanges from passage (5):

13. $A^1$ (i): I [wonder] whether the READER *recognised* the *sexual symbolism*.

   (ii): *James hates* his [father].

   $B^1$: But there's a RECONCILIATION.

   $A^2$: It's this *Oedipus* [thing].

   $C^1$: The [lighthouse] DOES [raise] [questions] about [symbols].

   $B^2$: I don't *see* ANY of these [sexual] [symbols].

We can give an approximate semantic and emphatic analysis of (13) as follows:

14. $A^1$  (i): ((I)((ASK(QUESTION$_a$))SELF(a(READER)RECOGNISE((SEXUAL)(SYMBOLS))))

| By (7a) | F | F | F | F | F | F | F | F |
|---|---|---|---|---|---|---|---|---|
| By (7b) | R | R | R | R | R | F | F | F |
| By (7c) | R | R | R | R | C | F | F | F |
| By (10) | | R | | | | | | |

 (ii): ((JAMES$_b$) −EMOTION (FATHER$_c$ −OF −b))$_d$

| By (7a) | F | F | F |
|---|---|---|---|
| By (7b) | F | F | R |

$B^1$: (~d)((△)BE((+EMOTION(b,c))$_e$ ∧(BECOME(e)(AGAIN))))

| By (7a) | F | F | | F | F |
|---|---|---|---|---|---|
| By (7b) | R | R | | F | F |
| By (7c) | R | C | | F | F |
| By (10) | R | | C | | |

$A^2$: ((d)BE((OEDIPUS)THING))

| By (7a) | F | F | F |
|---|---|---|---|
| By (7b) | R | F | R |

$C^1$: ((LIGHTHOUSE)(NOT−(~d))RAISE(QUESTIONS$_f$(fBE−ABOUT(SYMBOLS))))

| By (7a) | F | F | F | F | F | F |
|---|---|---|---|---|---|---|
| By (7b) | R | R | R | R | R | R |
| By (7c) | R | C | R | R | R | R |

$B^2$: ((I)SEE(NOT−ONE((SEXUAL)SYMBOL)))

| By (7a) | F | F | F | F | F |
|---|---|---|---|---|---|
| By (7b) | R | F | R | R | R |
| By (7c) | R | F | C | R | R |

A few points of this analysis require explanation. On the semantic structure suggested, notice that anaphors appear as variables bound by indices attached to their antecedents; this is so whether the antecedent is a nominal, a verbal or a sentential element. The adversativity of $B^1$ is represented as (~d), i.e. the negation of $A^1$; however, I have neglected to show explicitly the connection between this and the rest of $B^1$, which is presumably a justificatory connective ('I deny d because . . .'). Similarly, I have taken the contrastive positive polarity of $C^1$ to indicate disagreement with the adversative position of $B^1$: in this case the negative appears as a predicate, and ultimately as a stressed lexical item. Of the predicates used, ±EMOTION is borrowed from Leech (1969).

On the application of rule (7b), [wonder] in $A^1$ (i) actually represents a class of items which behave rather mysteriously. They are the 'verbs of propositional attitude' functioning as performatives, and the problem is that, while they are presumably content items, they behave with regard to emphasis like function items. We must assume that they belong to the automatically reduced 'conventionally recessive' items. This mystery is discussed in Werth (forthcoming: ch. 2). (FATHER) in $A^1$ (ii) is reduced here since it was previously mentioned, actually before our extract begins:

15. There's a family of children, and the youngest of them, James, longs to visit the lighthouse, and his mother says, 'Yes, if it's fine tomorrow, alright'. 'No, it won't be fine', says his father.

In $B^1$, (BE) is reduced by convention, while (+EMOTION) is reduced since it shares the predicate feature of (−EMOTION) in $A^1$. In $A^2$, (BE) and (THING) are both conventionally reduced. In $C^1$, (LIGHTHOUSE) and (SYMBOLS) are both actual repetitions, whereas (RAISE (QUESTIONS)) seems in some way to be suggested by [wonder] in $A^1$, which decomposes into something like ((ASK (QUESTION)) SELF); then (QUESTIONS) is directly repeated, while (RAISE) and (ASK) would be virtual synonyms in this instance. On rule (7c), (READER) in $A^1$ (i) is contrasted with (I), the speaker, while (+EMOTION) in $B^1$ denies (−EMOTION) in $A^1$ (ii), the whole item then becoming C by rule (10). The other cases have been discussed.

I am claiming, therefore, that relevance is the same as coherence. Speaker A introduces the question for general consideration, of whether the average reader recognises the sexual symbolism in the book (as he himself does). Since this contains a definite description, it bears a presupposition, namely that there is sexual symbolism throughout the book. (Of course, *the average reader* is also a definite NP, but not a definite description within the meaning of the act, since it is, presumably, generic.) Speaker A's presentation of this material is framed in such a way that the presupposition is more salient than the sentence which contains it: however, this seems to me to be an artefact. Stepping back from the logical viewpoint for a moment, and considering the communicative process, it seems to be the case that the speaker is introducing into the 'pending' file of the information pool the suggestion that there is sexual symbolism in the book. But to show its tentative nature, he hedges it in with *I wonder whether*, and couches it not as an assertion but apparently as a background assumption in a question about something else entirely: the average reader's perceptiveness. He then goes on to suggest in illustration of his real thesis that, among other things, James hates his father; speaker B denies this proposition by selecting one of its predicates, and reversing its polarity (this is embedded in a more complex expression which corresponds to a single lexical item). The denied item (ultimately, the word which contains it) is marked C. Speaker A, however, ignores this contradiction (i.e. he refuses to acknowledge that speaker B has challenged the incrementation of the information pool by the proposition that James hates his father; he simply assumes blithely that it has gone through). He merely adds some further information which coheres pragmatically with (FREUD), (HATE (FATHER)) etc. – though I have no idea how to represent this. Speaker C, though, *does* take B's objection into account; however, he is no more inclined to accept it than is A. In fact, he accepts A's earlier claim about the presence of sexual symbols (and he does not deny that James hates his father, either). Unlike A, however, he does at least acknowledge that B has lodged an objection (represented here by the repeated ($\sim$d)), which he then denies. Speaker B then reacts in a somewhat ambiguous way: she could be accepting the 'pending' proposition that there are sexual symbols, while complaining of her inability to see them; or she could be denying the proposition by way of a process which maintains: 'If I don't see a thing, it's not there'. The subsequent development of the conversation suggests that the former of these is correct, since she at least abandons her objections to A's proposition. This illustrates, if nothing else, that the incrementation of propositions is not necessarily a smooth rubber-stamp process, and that the notion of a pending file has some practical value.

Finally, let us briefly consider how the Wilson and Sperber (1979) proposals for ordered entailments fare, using this same material (which is much more complex than their own examples), and also to what extent they are simply equivalent to the analysis I have suggested above. First, they present an analysis of a sentence containing a contrastive stress, whose effect they claim (p. 315) is to narrow down the possible range of entailments contributing to relevance, whereas ordinary nuclear stress steers the hearer 'towards selection of one of the larger possible constituents as focus' (p. 315). This, however, is a practical effect: the entailments involved are identical. (A practical problem, as I show in Werth, forthcoming: ch. 2, is that there is no necessary superficial difference between contrast and what I call focus: contrast, as I have claimed, is a *semantic* relationship realised in various possible ways in the superficial linguistic expression, including stress, but also various types of movement, or linear ordering.)

However, let us take the simplified sentences of (13) in turn, and consider their entailments. First, $A^1$ (i) which contains C on *reader*:

16. (a) I wonder whether someone recognised the sexual symbolism
    (b) I wonder whether something was the case

Since the nucleus is contrastive, (16a) constitutes the background. The main point of the utterance, according to Wilson and Sperber, can be estimated by adding to the background whatever information is necessary to obtain $A^1$ (i), namely 'reader'. This is not in fact very convincing, and it would appear that having:

16. (c) I wonder whether the READER recognised something

as a background accords better with our intuitions that the correct incrementation here is 'the sexual symbolism'. Wilson and Sperber's account is thus very unsatisfactory at this point, though probably no less satisfactory than the conventional truth-conditional analysis based on the main clause. I should add, however, that the presuppositional behaviour of this sentence is complicated by its performative structure, and that although taking (16c) as background gets the incrementation right, it does not seem to throw much light on the presupposition of existence. Perhaps the problem is that, in communicative terms, speaker A is doing several things at once:

(i) expressing, or purporting to express, his tentativeness (*I wonder* . . .);
(ii) conveying his own perceptiveness, in possible contrast to that of the average reader (possible contrast only, since it is in the complement of *I wonder*);
(iii) suggesting the existence of sexual symbolism in the book, though again the construction makes this proposition presupposed rather than asserted.

He *seems* to be saying: 'There is sexual symbolism; I recognise it; Did the average reader?' He is *really* saying: 'I put it to you that there is sexual symbolism; I wonder if any other readers have recognised this.'

$A^1$ (ii), we know, is one of a number of illustrative examples of $A^1$ (i), a connection which is not made explicit in (14). Furthermore, in the coherence account, the thematic connection is of the difficult 'conceptual-sphere' type which we can do no more than describe at present. The entailments of $A^1$ (ii) are (assuming that *hates* is the nucleus):

17. (a) James does something in respect of his father
    (b) James does something in respect of something of his
    (c) James does something

Of these, it is presumably (17c) that is the background, which makes the point of $A^1$ (ii), by the Wilson-Sperber approach, 'hates his father'. The result seems intuitively correct, since it is the whole predicate (−EMOTION (FATHER)) which stands as an example of Freudian symbolism.

$B^1$ stands as a denial of $A^1$ (ii). Since it bears contrastive stress, Wilson and Sperber predict a narrow focus − however, there is little scope for anything else in this short sentence. The single entailment is:

18. There is something

The point of $B^1$ is thus shown to be 'a reconciliation', which is no surprise, but of course provides no insight either: that is, it tells us what the *locus* of relevance is, but provides no explanation for the actual connection made. In this case, the coherence account provides the necessary extra dimension.

$A^2$, as we have seen, completely ignores $B^1$, and represents in fact an extension of $A^1$ (ii), anaphorically bound to it by the pronominal subject. It has (non-contrastive) focus on *Oedipus*, giving entailments as follows:

19. (a) It's this some kind of thing
    (b) It's something

Going on our experience with the adjective phrase in $A^1$ (i), we should probably prefer (19b) as the background, making the incrementation 'this Oedipus thing'. Again, this does not seem very informative, but then the coherençe account is no better, since the coherence again depends on 'conceptual-sphere' information. A slight problem for the Wilson-Sperber account is that there is really very little difference between (19a) and (19b), thanks to the presence of the generalised noun *thing*.

$C^1$ responds positively to $A^1$ (i) and negatively to $B^1$. It contains a contrastive stress, so should have a narrow focus; in this case, though, that particular prediction does not seem to be borne out. Furthermore, the sentence raises problems for the Wilson-Sperber analysis which are syntactic in nature, since the statement of entailments depends upon a constituent division which is debatable:

20.  (a)  The lighthouse does do something
     (b)  The lighthouse does something
     (c)  ??The lighthouse sort of raises questions . . .

None of these constitutes an appropriate background for obtaining the correct incrementation, so in this case the Wilson-Sperber approach fails completely, whereas the coherence account can apparently handle it. Evidently, there is no variable of the right type to substitute for the contrast here.

Lastly, we come to $B^2$, which is a response to $A^1$ (i), and its evident acceptance by speaker C. The ambiguity of the utterance, discussed previously, can be handled in the informal presentation of variable substitution as:

21.  (a)  I don't see something
     (b)  I don't see anything

but the more specific entailment, suggested by the contrastive stress, is:

21.  (c)  I don't see some quantity of these sexual symbols.

Both (21a) and (21c) presuppose that there is something to see. If (21c) is the background, then the increment is 'any' or 'none', which is problematic for the seemingly intuitive relevance of $B^2$, namely the speaker's professed lack of perspicacity with regard to the sexual symbols accepted by the others. In other words, the 'point' of $B^2$ seems to be contained in its background entailment.

It appears, therefore, that there are are some problems for the ordered entailments account when it is unsupported by a measure of coherence. However, the analysis into background entailment and focal range etc. can provide a useful means of revealing the incrementing elements in a sentence, though the coherence account appears to go further in explaining — spelling out — the relevance of the sentence in terms of its context.

To sum up, then: current accounts of conversational interaction depend crucially upon the undefined notion of 'relevance'. This turns out to mean 'the appropriateness of an utterance-meaning to the meaning of the previous utterance, together with the context in which both occur'. This is therefore equivalent to the notion of **coherence**, i.e. 'complete or partial synonymy or coinciding implications'. The participants in a conversation keep track of coherence, and this is manifested in their use of the machinery of **emphasis-placement**, by which non-anaphoric items are focused, positively anaphoric items are reduced, and negatively anaphoric items are contrastive. Complete or partial synonymy can be handled by a **coherence-constraint** which keeps track of complete or partial similarity of semantic structure between antecedent and anaphoric element, while at least some cases of implicational coherence benefit from the machinery of **ordered entailments** proposed by Wilson and Sperber. Finally, another useful device which may turn out to be crucial is the notion of the **pending file** wherein propositions are stored while they are being negotiated.

## Notes

1. An approximate guide to this notation for emphasis is: *italics* (new information), [brackets] (repeated or predictable information), CAPITALS (contrast). A more exact characterisation follows later in the text.

2. I do not wish to get involved with problems of 'identity', 'reference' etc. in this paper, since they lead the discussion into areas rather remote from present concerns. However, in illustration of what I mean by 'identity', and to demonstrate that this is distinct from 'co-reference', consider the following case of the differently-treated adjective *beautiful* (which, being non-referential, cannot co-refer):

(i) *John* is *good-looking*. *Kate* is *beautiful*. (F: good looks and beauty are *different*)

(ii) *John* is *good-looking*. *Kate* is [beautiful] (too). (R: good looks and beauty are virtually the *same*)

(iii) *John* is *good-looking*. *Kate* is BEAUTIFUL (C: good looks and beauty are the *same sort of thing*, but beauty is *more besides*).

# References

Chomsky, N. (1972) 'Deep structure, surface structure, and semantic interpretation', in N. Chomsky *Studies on Semantics in Generative Grammar*, Mouton, The Hague

Gazdar, G. (1979) *Pragmatics: Implicature, Presupposition and Logical Form*, Academic Press, New York

Grice, H.P. (1975) 'Logic and conversation', in P. Cole and J.L. Morgan (eds.) *Syntax and semantics, 3: Speech Acts*, Academic Press, New York

—— (1978) 'Further notes on logic and conversation', in P. Cole (ed.) *Syntax and Semantics, 9: Pragmatics*, Academic Press, New York

Halliday, M.A.K. and R. Hasan (1976) *Cohesion in English*, Longman, London

Hankamer, J. and I. Sag (1976) 'Deep and surface anaphora', in *Linguistic Inquiry*, 7

Huddleston, R. (1978) 'On classifying anaphoric relations' in *Lingua*, 45

Jackendoff, R.S. (1972) *Semantic Interpretation in Generative Grammar*, M.I.T. Press, Cambridge, Mass.

Karttunen, L. (1977) 'Presupposition and linguistic context', in A. Rogers, B. Wall and J.P. Murphy (eds.) *Proceedings of the Texas Conference on Performatives, Presuppositions and Implicatures*, Center for Applied Linguistics, Arlington, Va.

—— and S. Peters (1979) 'Conventional implicature' in C-K. Oh and D.A. Dinneen (eds.) *Syntax and Semantics, 11: Presupposition*, Academic Press, New York

Lyons, J. (1977) *Semantics 1 and 2*, C.U.P., London

Leech, G. (1969) *Towards a Semantic Description of English*, Longman, London

McCawley, J.D. (1979) 'Presupposition and discourse structure' in C-K. Oh and D.A. Dinneen (eds.) *Syntax and Semantics, 11: Presupposition*, Academic Press, New York

Sacks, H., E. Schegloff, and G. Jefferson (1974) 'A simplest systematics for the organization of turn-taking for conversation' in *Language, 50*

Van Dijk, T.A. (1972) *Aspects of Text Grammars*, Mouton, The Hague

Wilson, D. and D. Sperber (1978) 'On Grice's theory of conversation', in *Pragmatics Microfiche, 3.5* (reprinted in this volume)

—— —— (1979) 'Ordered entailments: an alternative to presuppositional theories', in C-K. Oh and D.A. Dinneen (eds.) *Syntax and Semantics, 11: Presupposition*, Academic Press, New York

Werth, P.N. (1980) 'Articles of association: determiners and context', in J. van der Auwera (ed.) *The Semantics of Determiners*, Croom Helm, London

—— (forthcoming) *Focus and Grammar*, Croom Helm, London

# 8 ON GRICE'S THEORY OF CONVERSATION*

### Deirdre Wilson and Dan Sperber

It is now ten years since Paul Grice, in his William James Lectures, laid down the foundations for a theory of conversation.[1] Although the full text of these lectures has never been published, Grice's views have had considerable influence on most recent approaches to pragmatics. Following Grice, conversation is now generally conceived of as a co-operative venture, governed by maxims of truthfulness, relevance, informativeness and manner, which may be exploited for particular conversational effects.[2] A distinction between what the speaker explicitly said and what he tacitly implied or implicated, and a classification of implicatures into various types, are now part of the standard machinery for pragmatic analysis. Although specific proposals have been made for extending, supplementing or modifying Grice's machinery, it seems no exaggeration to say that most recent theories of utterance-interpretation are a direct result of Grice's William James Lectures.[3]

The value of Grice's work derives not so much from the detail of his analyses as from the general claim that underlies them. Grice has shown that given an adequate set of pragmatic principles — to which his conversational maxims are a first approximation — a wide range of what at first sight seem to be arbitrary semantic facts can be seen as consequences of quite general pragmatic constraints. The broad outline of this position is extremely convincing, and we have relied on it in our own recent research. However, it seems to us that its detail needs considerable modification if any further progress is to be made. In this paper, we shall assume that the advantages of a Gricean approach are well enough known to need no further comment, and concentrate instead on three main areas of dissatisfaction. First, we shall argue that the distinction between saying and implicating is not as simple as Grice suggests, and that the hearer uses Grice's maxims not only in deciding what has been implicated, but also in deciding what proposition has actually been expressed. Secondly, we shall argue that there is more to the interpretation of such figures as irony and metaphor than a mere knowledge of the maxims of conversation, although Grice seems to suggest that there is not. Thirdly, we shall take up the notion of implicature itself, and go on to argue that the maxims are not all independently necessary for the generation of implicatures: that they may in fact be

155

reduced to a single principle, which we call the principle of relevance. The resulting account, while it differs considerably from Grice's, seems to us to do greater justice to the processes involved in the interpretation of utterances.

## 1. The Role of Grice's Maxims in Determining What is Said

Grice seems to be attempting to provide a framework into which every aspect of the interpretation of an utterance can be fitted. He draws a major distinction between what is actually said and what is tacitly implicated, suggesting that every aspect of interpretation can be assigned to one or other category. What is said (in our terms, what proposition the utterance is taken to express) is largely determined by linguistic rule, while what is implicated is largely determined by social and other maxims. The implicatures are subclassified into various types, the most important being the conversational implicatures, governed by the conversational maxims. It seems to follow, within Grice's framework, that (a) the maxims play no role in determining what is said, and (b) any aspect of interpretation governed by the maxims must be analysable as a conversational implicature. In fact, neither of these claims seems to be true. We shall argue that while there is a valid distinction between the proposition expressed by an utterance and the conversational implicatures conveyed, the hearer uses Grice's maxims as much in determining what proposition has been expressed as in determining its conversational implicatures. In other words, the scope of the maxims, and of pragmatic theory, is wider than Grice thought, and the semantics-pragmatics distinction cannot be reduced to a distinction between saying and implicating.

As Grice points out, in order to know what the speaker actually said on a given occasion of utterance, two things are necessary: first, knowledge of the range of possible senses of the utterance and its range of possible referents; and secondly, a decision about which sense and reference the speaker intended it to have on that particular occasion. Now while the first of these is explicitly given by semantic rules, the second is not. What Grice fails to notice is that the maxims of conversation play just as great a role in determining this second, context-sensitive aspect of what is said as they do in working out the conversational implicatures of an utterance. In other words, the distinction between saying and implicating is not co-extensive with the semantics-pragmatics distinction, and neither corresponds exactly to the distinction between explicitly and implicitly given information.

Consider the following utterance:

(1)  Refuse to admit them.

In Grice's terms, (1) has at least two possible senses, depending on whether *admit* means 'let in' or 'confess to'. It also has an indefinite range of possible referents, since *them* could refer to any group of people or objects known to speaker and hearer. Now imagine that (1) is said in response to (2):

(2)  What should I do when I make mistakes?

Interpreting (1) in this context, the hearer can immediately eliminate all of the possible interpretations of (1) except the one in which *admit* means 'confess to' and *them* refers to the speaker's mistakes. When (1) is said in response to (3), the interpretation changes considerably:

(3)  What should I do with the people whose tickets have expired?

Here, *admit* will be interpreted as meaning 'let in', and *them* as referring to the people whose tickets have expired. In considering how these interpretations are achieved, there is an obvious point to make. Whatever the context, (1) still has an indefinite range of logically possible interpretations, any one of which could have been intended by a speaker who was not observing Grice's maxims. It seems clear that the hearer's ability to select the appropriate interpretation for (1) in the context of (2) or (3) must depend on his tacit assumption that the speaker has observed Grice's maxims, and in particular the maxim of relevance. He can then eliminate any interpretation which does not accord with this assumption. In other words, at least two aspects of what is said (what proposition is expressed) — disambiguation and the assignment of reference — are not semantically but pragmatically determined: they are not explicitly given by semantic rule but implicitly determined by context and the maxim of relevance. The semantics-pragmatics distinction cross-cuts the distinction between saying and implicating.

This in turn suggests the more general claim, to which we know of no serious counter-examples, that hearers invariably ascribe sense and reference to utterances (within the limits allowed by the grammar) in such a way as to preserve their assumption that the conversational maxims have been observed. If this is true, the disambiguation of utterances, and the assignment of reference to their referring phrases, must fall squarely within the domain of pragmatics, and within the scope of the conversational maxims, contrary to what Grice appears to claim.[4] Pragmatics must be concerned with more than just the nonconventional implicatures of an utterance: it should also be able to account for certain implicit aspects of what is actually said.

Nor is it just disambiguation and the assignment of reference in which the maxims play a role. Quite often, they lead the hearer to ascribe to an utterance some propositional content that is not strictly warranted by semantic rules alone. Suppose John Smith is playing the violin in front of us, and I say to you:

(4)   John plays well.

In these circumstances, I would naturally be taken as having expressed the proposition in (5):

(5)   John Smith plays the violin well.

The fact that *John* is taken as referring to John Smith, and that *play* is taken as meaning 'play a musical instrument' rather than 'play a game', has already been accounted for. The resulting proposition should be (6), where the missing direct object in (4) is semantically interpreted in terms of a specific indefinite phrase:

(6)   John plays some musical instrument well.

It is clear, though, that the hearer of (4) will normally interpret it as expressing not (6), but the more specific (5). We shall not attempt a full account of this fact here. Note, however, that (5) entails (6), so that whenever (5) is true (6) will also be true, but not vice-versa. (5) therefore has more chances of being informative than (6), and one can conceive of circumstances in which (5), but not (6), would satisfy the maxims of informativeness, and (5) would thus be preferred to (6). It seems clear that any adequate account of how (4) is interpreted as expressing (5) rather than (6) will have to appeal to the maxims of informativeness, and that these may lead the hearer to choose a more specific interpretation than is warranted by the semantic rules alone.

Grice's framework forces us to ask whether in cases like the above the speaker of (4) SAID (5), or merely implicated it. Neither answer seems to be entirely adequate. On the one hand, the speaker of (4) can deny without contradiction that he meant (5) — as in (7), for example:

(7)   John plays well — he just doesn't play the VIOLIN well.

This suggests that (5) should be classed as a conversational implicature rather than part of what is said, since it is a defining property of conversational implicatures that they are always cancellable. However, disambiguation and the assignment of reference give rise to similar cancellable aspects of the interpretation of an utterance, which Grice explicitly claims form part of what is said. Moreover, if we want to maintain the intuitive distinction between the propositions expressed by an utterance and the implicatures worked out on the basis of the propositions expressed, then (5) does not fall at all naturally into the class of conversational implicatures, since it is on the basis of (5) rather than (6) that the implicatures of (4) will be worked out. Within Grice's framework there will thus be certain aspects of interpretation that cannot be satisfactorily classified: they are not explicitly given by semantic rule, but they are not conversational implicatures either. Rather than distinguishing, as Grice does, between what is explicitly said and what is tacitly implicated, it would be more satisfactory to distinguish, as we have been suggesting, between the proposition the speaker is taken to have expressed — partly explicitly, partly implicitly — and the deductions of various types which can be drawn from it. The conversational maxims, and in particular the maxim of relevance, have a role to play in both aspects of interpretation.[5]

The main purpose of this section has been to show that Grice's fundamental distinction between what is said (as given by semantic rules) and what is conversationally implicated (as given by the conversational maxims) is neither exclusive nor exhaustive. The maxims play a role in disambiguation, the assignment of reference and, more generally, in determining the proposition expressed by an utterance as well as its conversational implicatures. If he fails to invoke the maxim of relevance in particular, the hearer will not only miss the subtler implications of an utterance; quite often he will have no idea what was actually being said. In this respect at least, the scope of the maxims, and hence of pragmatic theory, is wider than Grice thought.

## 2. The Role of the Maxims in the Interpretation of Figurative Utterances

Grice claims that irony, metaphor, meiosis (understatement) and hyperbole can all be analysed in terms of conversational implicatures. Not only that, they all result from violation of the same maxim: 'Do not say what you believe to be false'. In other words, the salient feature of figurative utterances, as Grice sees them, is that they are patently false. According to Grice, the hearer concludes that the speaker must have been attempting to get across some closely related proposition which does not violate the maxim of truthfulness: in the case of irony, for example, it might be the contradictory of the proposition uttered, and in the case of metaphor it might be a comparison, so that a metaphor is reinterpreted as implicating a simile. Grice makes no suggestion about which related propositions would be conveyed by meiosis or hyperbole; however, in the case of meiosis it might be a strengthened version of the proposition expressed by an utterance, and in the case of hyperbole a weakened version. The originality of this approach lies mainly in its attempt to incorporate traditional rhetorical ideas into a modern theory of pragmatics. However, the attempt seems to us to raise a number of new problems, while failing to provide solutions to many of those already in existence.

In most of the examples of conversational implicature that Grice discusses, the speaker of an utterance intends to convey both what is conversationally implicated *and* what is actually said. In the case of metaphor, irony and so on, the speaker intends to convey only what is conversationally implicated: the conversational implicatures of the utterance thus have to be seen as cancelling what is actually said. This analysis seems to us to involve an unjustified extension of the notion of a conversational implicature. The basic rationale behind the notion of conversational implicature is that the hearer posits the existence of an implicature in order to preserve his assumption that the conversational maxims have been observed on the level of what is said. In the case of metaphor, irony and so on, the fact that an implicature has to be *substituted* for what was literally said ought to confirm the hearer's suspicion that the maxims have been violated, rather than preserving his assumption that they have been obeyed. In other words, the implicatures carried by irony, metaphor, etc. do not seem to be at all of the same type as more standard implicatures; they do not satisfy the same basic definition, and they must be worked out according to rather different principles.

The connection between Grice's conception of irony and metaphor and the traditional rhetorical view that certain utterances have 'figurative' as opposed to 'literal' meaning should be obvious. In both cases the interpretation of an utterance is claimed to involve the substitution of one type of conveyed meaning for another; in both cases the relations between 'literal' and 'figurative' meaning, and the rationale for substituting one for the other, remain unclear.

Grice claims that when faced with a blatant and deliberate falsehood, the hearer looks around for some proposition closely related to the one expressed, and interprets this as an implicature. One of the problems here is simply deciding what counts as a 'closely related proposition', one which could be got across by a figure of speech. Given that there are figures based on contradiction and comparison, for example, why not also a figure based on reversal of subject and object roles, so that where *Peter loves Mary* is patently false, it is taken as implicating *Mary loves Peter*? There is a vast range of similar logical relationships among propositions which are never called on in the interpretation of utterances.[6] This strongly suggests that it is not logical factors alone, but also other psychological factors, that govern our perception of relationships among propositions. Certain such relationships spring immediately to mind, while others, just as obvious from the logical point of view, are simply never noticed.

Even given that certain patently false utterances are interpreted as implicating their contradictories, others as implicating related similes, and so on, it would still be a mystery, in Grice's framework, why not all patently false utterances are figuratively interpreted. If Grice's account of figurative speech is correct, it should always be possible, for example, to hand someone a £5 note and say (8), knowing that it will be interpreted as ironical:

(8)  This is not a £5 note.

In the same circumstances, (9) should always be capable of metaphorical interpretation, (10) of interpretation as meiosis, and (11) of interpretation as hyperbole:

(9)  This is a 5 yen note.
(10)  This is a £3 note.
(11)  This is a £20 note.

Obviously, in the absence of special circumstances, if the falsehoods in (8)–(11) are explicable at all, they would be taken as mistakes, jokes or irrelevancies, rather than as figurative uses of language.[7]

The above examples show that violation of the maxim of truthfulness is not a sufficient condition for figurative interpretation. In fact, it is not necessary either. This should be obvious enough in the case of meiosis, which is generally truthful but not informative enough, as where (12) is said of a goalkeeper who has let in twelve or fourteen goals:

(12)　It's not his best game ever.

But in addition, ironical declaratives such as (13) and hyperbolical declaratives such as (14) have as counterparts such questions as (15) and (16); these retain their figurative character even though there can be no question of their violating the maxim of truthfulness.

(13)　Hector's a genius.
(14)　No-one could be nicer than Stella.
(15)　a. Isn't Hector a genius?
　　　　b. Is Hector a genius?
(16)　Who could be nicer than Stella?

It is true that (15) and (16) can be interpreted as 'rhetorical questions', which simultaneously implicate and ask a question about their related declaratives (13) and (14). The irony in (15) and the hyperbole in (16) could then be linked to the fact that the alleged implicatures in (13) and (14) are patent violations of the maxim of truthfulness. But such an account, however plausible, is incompatible with Grice's framework. In Grice's framework, the hearer looks for an interpretation which conforms to the maxims, and only introduces an implicature in order to arrive at such an interpretation. Now (15) and (16) can perfectly well be understood as non-rhetorical questions which carry no implicatures at all. Moreover, to interpret (15) as implicating (13), and (16) as implicating (14), is to *introduce* a violation of the maxims, rather than getting rid of one, since by hypothesis, in these figurative cases, (13) and (14) would be literally false. Nothing in Grice's framework appears to justify such a move.

Given a metaphor such as (17), there is always a related question such as (18) and a related declarative such as (19), both of which would be interpreted metaphorically even though they do not violate the maxim of truthfulness:

(17)　Her mother is an angel.
(18)　Isn't her mother an angel?
(19)　Her mother is no angel.

It would, of course, be possible to persist in the claim that figurative utterances always result from violation of one of the maxims. But as is shown by (12), (15), (16), (18) and (19), it is just as likely to be a violation of informativeness or relevance as a violation of truthfulness that gives rise to figurative interpretation. It does not seem that any particular one of Grice's maxims should be given a privileged position in a unified account of figurative language.

Grice's account of figurative language seems inadequate in some respects and mistaken in others. The most serious objection to his account is that the interpretation of a figurative utterance cannot be reduced to the mere search for an appropriate implicature. The interpretation of an utterance may be regarded as a set of propositions: as we have seen, some of these are propositions expressed by the utterance, while others are implicated by it. However, in addition to the propositions it expresses or implicates, an utterance may suggest to the hearer certain non-propositional lines of interpretation — for example by evoking images or states of mind — which are precisely characteristic of figurative utterances, and which cannot be analysed within Grice's framework at all.

Grice probably has these aspects of interpretation in mind at the end of *Logic and Conversation* (1975), when he suggests that an utterance may implicate, not a specific proposition, but an open-ended disjunction of propositions. However, he defines implicatures as premises in an argument designed to preserve the hearer's assumption that the maxims have been obeyed, and an open-ended disjunction of propositions can never be a premise in a valid argument. What this suggests is that some other process, quite distinct from implicature, is at work in figurative interpretation. Instead of saying that a figurative utterance implicates an open-ended disjunction of propositions, we shall say that it **evokes** a range of propositions, possibly interspersed with images.

To take a concrete example, consider Grice's case of meiosis: the remark in (20) applied to someone known to have broken up all the furniture:

(20) He was a little intoxicated.

What makes (20) figurative is precisely that it does not simply implicate a proposition closely related to the one litally expressed. In particular, it is not merely equivalent to (21), as we believe Grice wants to suggest:

(21) He was exceedingly drunk.

As well as implicating something like (21), (20) calls to mind, as (21) does not, a world in which it *would* be considered appropriate to utter (20) of a man in an advanced state of drunkenness; a world, perhaps, in which the full extremes of drunkenness and violence are much more commonly encountered, and have much more notable consequences. Alternatively, (20) might evoke, as (21) does not, an image of its speaker as a man of such unassailable stoicism and imperturbability that even violent drunkenness fails to move him. In either case, (20) does much more than merely implicating (21) — not because it carries other, equally specific implicatures, but rather because it evokes an indefinite range of conjectures and images.

Thus, while Grice underestimated the scope of the maxims in the case of saying versus implicating, he seems to have overestimated it in the case of figurative interpretation. What seems to be needed is a new type of interpretive mechanism, in addition to the semantic and pragmatic ones already available, which can account for irony, metaphor, and figurative interpretation in general. Considerable progress has been made, largely thanks to Grice, by relieving semantics of a number of problems which were better handled within an improved theory of pragmatics; it now seems that if pragmatics is to progress further, it will have to be relieved in turn of a number of problems which cannot be handled in purely grammatical or logical terms, and demand treatment within a separate theory of rhetoric.[8]

## 3. Conversational Implicatures and the Reduction of Grice's Maxims

Grice defines a conversational implicature as a proposition which the hearer must take the speaker to believe, in order to preserve his assumption that the Co-Operative Principle and maxims have been obeyed. Such implicatures, although often intuitively grasped, must also, Grice says, be capable of being explicitly worked out: by this he presumably means that they are deducible on some basis from the content of the utterance and the fact that it was made. There are a number of ways of construing this definition, and the examples of conversational implicature that Grice gives do not always point to a unique construal. In this section, we shall choose a fairly narrow construal, but our main purpose will be to show that Grice's fundamental distinction between saying and implicating obscures a number of aspects of utterance-interpretation, and to provide a more satisfactory account. In this new account, conversational implicatures will play a central role, but will by no means exhaust the propositions contributed by the pragmatic interpretation process.

Consider question (22) and the range of possible answers in (23a–d):

(22) Do you ever talk to Charles?
(23) a. No, I never talk to him.
     b. He is a philosopher, and I never talk to philosophers.
     c. I never talk to philosophers.
     d. I never talk to plagiarists.

Assume that in (23a–d) the hearer construes the referring phrases *he/him* and *I* along the lines suggested in section 1: in accordance with the maxim of relevance. Assume also that it has already been established between the speaker and hearer of (23c) that Charles is a philosopher, but that it has not been similarly established for (23d) that Charles is a plagiarist. In these circumstances, each of (23a–d) may be construed as conveying the answer (24) to (22):

(24) The speaker of (23) never talks to Charles.

In virtue of this, each of (23a–d) is a relevant response to (22); however, it is intuitively clear that each is less direct than the preceding one, in the sense that each requires the hearer to do more work in arriving at the conclusion (24).

In the circumstances just outlined, (24) is directly expressed by (23a). While not directly expressed by (23b), it is deducible from (23b) given standard rules of deduction. While not deducible from (23c) alone, it is deducible from (23c) together with premise (25), which we are assuming to be an established part of shared knowledge:

(25) Charles is a philosopher.

Finally, while (24) is neither expressed by (23d) nor deducible from it in any of the ways just mentioned, it would be so deducible if the extra premise in (26) could be added to shared knowledge:

(26) Charles is a plagiarist.

The increasing indirectness of the responses in (23a–d) can thus be correlated with the amount of work each requires from the hearer in order to arrive at (24). (23a) requires him to do no work beyond establishing which proposition is expressed by the utterance; (23b) requires him to do this, and also to draw a deduction from the proposition expressed; (23c) requires him first to retrieve a proposition from his memory store, and then to draw a deduction from the proposition retrieved, together with the proposition expressed by the utterance; and (23d) requires him to construct, rather than retrieve, a certain proposition, and then to draw a deduction from it, together with the proposition expressed. A framework which provided an account of these facts would be able to reconstruct the intuitive notion of 'indirectness of response' in the way just outlined.

It is clear from the account of (23a–d) just given that the process of utterance-interpretation is essentially a deductive one, and that the elements involved in the deduction are:

(a) the propositional content of the utterance
(b) items of the hearer's background knowledge
(c) a set of inference rules
(d) the maxims of conversation.

In the case of (23a–c) the deductive process is a straightforward one, with the maxims, and in particular the maxim of relevance, playing no role apart from constraining input and output propositions: selecting the relevant premises, and determining when a relevant conclusion has been reached. We shall argue that the interpretation of (23d) is also straightforwardly deductive, but that the assumption that the speaker has observed the maxim of relevance itself occurs as a crucial premise in the deduction.

Part of the hearer's background knowledge will derive from the fact that a certain utterance has been made, and the circumstances and manner in which it was made. Knowledge of this type is contributed by every utterance, not in virtue of its content, but in virtue of its context and style. In the case of (23a–c) knowledge of this type plays no crucial role in the interpretive process, but in the case of (23d) it seems that it must play such a role.

When the content of the utterance alone does not suffice to establish its relevance, as it does not in the case of (23d), a hearer who assumes that the conversational maxims have been observed may introduce as one of the premises in his deduction the fact that it was said, and said in a particular manner, perhaps in response to other remarks. In the case of (23d) he might reason as follows. (23d) was said in a manner which does not suggest that the speaker was opting out of the maxim of relevance, and said in response to question (22). (22) is itself a yes-no question, and a maximally relevant response to it will entail either (24) or its negation (27):

(27)   The speaker of (23d) sometimes talks to Charles.

To establish the relevance of (23d), its hearer must thus supply premises which, together with the content of (23d), will entail either (24) or (27). The additional premise that Charles is a plagiarist, together with the content of (23d), entails (24), and would therefore establish the relevance of the utterance. If the speaker can find no other such premise, and can find none that would combine with (23d) to yield (27), then it follows that *only* with this additional premise can the relevance of (23d) be established. On the assumption that the maxim of relevance has been observed, it will then follow logically that Charles is a plagiarist – or that the speaker of (23d) wants the hearer to think so. In this way, the additional premise is deducible, not from the content of (23d) alone, but from its content together with the fact that it has been made in certain circumstances, and from the maxim of relevance itself. Given the additional premise, he can then proceed to the conclusion that the speaker of (23d) never talks to Charles, and so establish the relevance of the utterance.

According to the account just given, the interpretation of the utterances in (23a–d) proceeds in essentially the same fashion. In each case, the hearer tries to establish the relevance of the utterance by deducing either (24) or (27). In the case of (23a–b), items of background knowledge are used only in deciding what proposition the utterance expresses. In the case of (23c), a crucial premise must be supplied from the hearer's background knowledge, and in the case of (23d) a crucial premise must itself be deduced in the way outlined above. We suggest the following terminology for distinguishing the four separate cases: (23a) **expresses** (24); the proposition expressed by (23b) **logically implies** (24); and (23c) and (23d) both **pragmatically imply** (24), where pragmatic implication is defined as follows:

(28)   A proposition P pragmatically implies a proposition Q if f:
   (a) P, together with other premises M, supplied by the hearer, logically implies Q
   (b) P does not logically imply Q
   (c) M does not logically imply Q.[9]

Where the pragmatic implication follows from the content of the utterance and the hearer's background knowledge alone, as in the case of (23c), we shall call it a **direct** pragmatic implication; where an additional premise, not part of the hearer's background knowledge, has to be supplied, as in the case of (23d), we shall call it an **additional premise**; and the pragmatic implications which follow from additional premises and the maxim of relevance, as in the case of (23d), we shall call **indirect** pragmatic implications.

It is an open question which of the categories defined above Grice would regard as conversational implicatures. Broadly speaking, direct and indirect pragmatic implications and additional premises could all be seen as conversational implicatures; but the essential differences between them would then be obscured. A narrower construal is suggested by two facts: first, Grice continually refers to conversational implicatures as premises rather than conclusions in a deductive process; and secondly, he continually refers to them as deriving from the fact that the utterance was made rather than its propositional content alone. Given this, the most plausible assumption is that Grice intended conversational implicatures to be co-extensive with what we have been calling additional premises. If this is so, it follows, as we have suggested above, that the distinction between saying and conversationally implicating is very far from exhausting all aspects of utterance interpretation: there is no place in Grice's framework for the categories of direct and indirect pragmatic implications, which play a crucial role in interpretation.

As a result of these omissions, it seems to us that Grice has deprived himself of the necessary tools for defining relevance. We shall argue that the relevance of an utterance can be assessed in terms of its pragmatic implications, both direct and indirect; we would also claim that additional premises contribute only indirectly to the relevance of an utterance, via the indirect pragmatic implications they bring along with them. A framework with no explicit place for pragmatic implications is thus a framework which lacks the categories necessary for defining relevance.

On an extremely intuitive level, the more pragmatic implications an utterance has, the more relevant it is. This needs some qualification: of two utterances which are equally rich in semantic content, it will be the one with more pragmatic implications that is also more relevant; however, of two utterances which are equally rich in pragmatic implications, it will be the one with *less* semantic content that is also more relevant. For example, if (29) has more pragmatic implications than (30), it is (29) that will be more relevant:

(29) The girl Bill saw yesterday works as a part-time cashier in a bank.

(30) The girl Bill saw yesterday works in a bank.

On the other hand, if (29) and (30) have the same number of pragmatic implications, it is (30) rather than (29) that will be more relevant. In other words, if the information that the girl referred to is a part-time cashier contributes to the pragmatic implications of (29), then (29) will be more relevant than (30); on the other hand, if this information contributes no pragmatic implications at all, this will *detract* from the relevance of the utterance, so that (30) will be more relevant than (29).

Because of the connection between pragmatic implications and background assumptions, two different hearers with different beliefs and assumptions will not always draw the same pragmatic implications from a given utterance, and will thus not perceive its relevance in the same way. A single hearer at different times and in different circumstances will bring different beliefs and assumptions to bear on the interpretation of an utterance, and in this case too, his judgements of relevance may vary. In general, the relevance of an utterance is established relative to a set of beliefs and assumptions – that is, a set of propositions; relevance is a relation between the proposition expressed by an utterance, on the one hand, and the set of propositions in the hearer's accessible memory on the other.

On a slightly more abstract level, the more pragmatic implications a proposition P has relative to a set of assumptions M, the more relevant P is to M. When two propositions P and Q have the same pragmatic implications relative to a set of assumptions M, the proposition with less semantic content is the more relevant to M.[10]

One of the factors affecting judgements of relevance will thus be the set of assumptions M brought to bear on the interpretation of an utterance. One of the tasks of pragmatic theory is to describe how a given utterance helps to determine the set of assumptions against which its relevance – and that of the following utterance – is to be assessed. We can state the problem a little more precisely. There are two fairly well-defined sets of propositions available to speaker and hearer at a given moment in conversation. On the one hand, there is the set consisting of the shared beliefs and assumptions of speaker and hearer which are actually accessible to them at that moment; on the other hand, there is the set of propositions which have been used in the interpretation of the preceding utterance, or which form part of its interpretation. In general, the set M against which the relevance of an utterance is assessed is included in the former set, and includes the latter. Depending on the nature of the conversation (reasoned argument or informal chat), on whether the previous remark came early or late in the development of an argument, and on whether this remark was a question or an answer, the preferred set of assumptions M will vary between its upper and lower limits. In any case, speaker and hearer have a certain latitude in interpretation, and the hearer must thus form some hypothesis about the contents of the set M against which the speaker intended his utterance to be relevant; this hypothesis will be affected by the factors just mentioned. It seems to us that, put in these terms, the problem of how M is actually determined on any given occasion is in principle capable of solution, and that the notion of relevance in context is thus not irremediably vague.

We can use this definition of relevance to provide the following account of how utterances are interpreted.

The hearer treats (31) as axiomatic:

(31)  The speaker has done his best to be maximally relevant.

The notion of 'doing one's best' will of course vary according to the type of conversation (cocktail party chat or academic seminar), and the amount of effort needed to establish the relevance of the utterance will also vary depending on the range of alternative hypotheses about the extent of M, the need for construction of additional premises, and so on. There will generally be several logically possible assignments of sense and reference to a given utterance: the hearer will choose the assignment which most clearly satisfies (31).

Taking the proposition thus expressed, together with a chosen set of assumptions M, the hearer proceeds to work out the direct pragmatic implications of the utterance. If there are enough of these to satisfy (31) above, the interpretation ends. If not, taking as his initial premises the fact and circumstances of utterance, the hearer attempts to construct additional premises. When these are added to M, indirect pragmatic implications may be obtained, and these, together with any direct pragmatic implications, may establish the relevance of the utterance. If this procedure fails, the rhetorical mechanisms of evocation are brought into play.

In other words, we are claiming that Grice's maxims can be replaced by a single **principle of relevance** (31). In interpreting an utterance the hearer uses this principle as a guide, on the one hand towards correct disambiguation and assignment of reference, and on the other in deciding whether additional premises are needed, and if so what they are, or whether a figurative interpretation was intended. The principle of relevance on its own provides an adequate, and we think rather more explicit, account of all the implicatures which Grice's maxims were set up to describe. We shall try to illustrate this taking each maxim in turn. The maxims of quantity (32a) and (32b) are particularly vague:

(32) a. Make your contribution as informative as is required (for the present purposes of the exchange).
   b. Do not make your contribution more informative than is required.

No clue is given about what constitutes the required level of informativeness. The principle of relevance subsumes both these maxims, and at the same time makes them more precise. If the speaker holds back some information which, together with M, would yield pragmatic implications, he is violating both the principle of relevance and maxim (32a). If he gives information which yields no pragmatic implications, he is violating both the principle of relevance and maxim (32b). Grice himself points out that the effect of (32b) is secured by his maxim of relevance. The effect of (32a) should be equally secured by a principle of *maximal* relevance, such as (31). Hence, in a system which contains (31), both maxims of quantity are redundant.

The maxims of quality (33a) and (33b) raise a number of problems, not all of which we shall go into here:

(33) a. Do not say what you believe to be false.
   b. Do not say that for which you lack adequate evidence.

As we said above, being relevant is a matter of inducing the hearer to expand or modify his set of initial beliefs or assumptions. Such expansion or modification is the result of a deductive process based on premises supplied by shared knowledge, the content of the utterance, and, if necessary, the fact that the utterance has been made, and the circumstances in which it was made. It should go without saying that the premises used in this deduction include only those which the hearer believes or assumes to be true: to establish the relevance of an utterance, the hearer has to make valid inferences from a set of premises which are true, or assumed to be true.

A speaker aiming to maximise relevance will generally succeed in doing so if he does his best to speak truthfully and on the basis of adequate evidence. Thus, in most cases, the principle of relevance subsumes the maxims of quality. However, there are certain cases in which the principle of relevance and Grice's maxims of quality make rather different predictions. For example, if (34) is said to a doctor by a patient who 'lacks adequate evidence', from Grice's point of view there will have been a violation of maxim (33b): the result should be a conversational implicature:

(34)  I'm ill.

From our point of view, the circumstances of utterance are such that if the remark is sincerely made, its relevance is guaranteed: the fact that the speaker was not competent to pronounce on whether he was ill or otherwise would have little effect on the implications of the utterance. In such cases, it seems to be the principle of relevance which makes the correct predictions.

The maxim of relation (35) is clearly subsumed under the principle of relevance:

(35)  Be relevant.

There remain only the maxims of manner, (36a–d):

(36)  a. Avoid obscurity of expression
      b. Avoid ambiguity.
      c. Be brief (avoid unnecessary prolixity).
      d. Be orderly.

(36a) obviously follows from the principle of relevance. Establishing the relevance of an utterance involves working out its pragmatic implications. This can only be done if the hearer knows which proposition has been expressed, and a speaker who talks obscurely runs the risk that the hearer will be unable to decide which proposition this is. Hence to speak obscurely is to violate the principle of relevance. (36b) is misplaced. In the first place, since virtually every utterance IS ambiguous, it seems that this maxim could never be satisfactorily obeyed. In the second place, there is in general no point in avoiding ambiguity, since, as we have argued, hearers normally select the interpretation on which the utterance would be most relevant. It is only in the rare cases where two senses of an utterance would be equally relevant that semantic ambiguity is accompanied by pragmatic equivocation.

Equivocation poses the same problem as obscurity of expression, and violates the principle of relevance in exactly the same way.

At the very least, maxim (36c) is misstated. The claim is that, given two utterances of different length which express the same propositions, it is always the shorter of the two that is the most appropriate. Apart from the fact that no clue is given how brevity should be measured (in terms of word-counts, syllable-counts, phrase-counts, syntactic or semantic complexity) the sentence-pairs in (37) and (38) clearly demonstrate that this claim is false:

(37)  a. Peter is married to Madeleine.
      b. It is Peter who is married to Madeleine.
(38)  a. Mary ate a peanut.
      b. Mary put a peanut into her mouth, chewed and swallowed it.

By any brevity-measure, the (a) member of these pairs is shorter than the (b) member. However, there are contexts in which the (b) member would be more appropriate, and where no conversational implicature would result from the consequent violation of the maxim of brevity.

In (37) and (38), the (a) and (b) members differ not in their logical implications, but in the relative importance assigned to them. By changing the linguistic form of his utterance – even at the expense of making it longer – the speaker can draw the hearer's attention to certain of its logical implications.[11] If these are the implications on which the relevance of the utterance depends, the speaker will then have done his best to indicate to the hearer how its relevance is to be established. This suggests the following corollary to the principle of relevance:

(39)  Where the linguistic form of an utterance draws attention to certain of its logical implications, these are the ones on which the relevance of the utterance depends.

Suppose that the speaker does not observe (39). Suppose, for example, that he says (40b) rather than (40a):

(40)  a. The baby is eating arsenic!
      b. The baby is putting arsenic into his mouth, chewing and swallowing it!

(40b) suggests, absurdly in the context, that certain aspects of the meaning of *eat* are particularly relevant to its interpretation. This is the real reason for its unacceptability: the fact that it is also longer than (40a) is incidental.

Maxim (36d) ('Be orderly') was set up mainly to explain contrasts of the following type:

(41)  a. Jenny sang, and Maria played the piano.
       b. Maria played the piano, and Jenny sang.

In certain contexts, (41a) and (41b) are pragmatically equivalent, carrying the same implications and implicatures. However, as Grice points out, there are also possible interpretations on which (41a) and (41b) impute different temporal or causal relations to their constituent propositions. (41a), for example, would suggest that Jenny sang before Maria played the piano, and (41b) would suggest the reverse order of events. The maxim of orderliness was designed to explain these facts without appeal to any semantic claim that *and* has an extra sense, equivalent to *and then* or *and so*. We think the contrast between (41a) and (41b) can indeed be explained without postulating an extra sense of *and*, but we also think it can be explained without postulating a special maxim or orderliness.

All we need is the assumption that the hearer may establish the relevance of a co-ordinate proposition in two different ways. Either he works out the pragmatic implications of the two constituent conjuncts on the basis of the same set of initial assumptions M; or the implications and implicatures of the first conjunct are added to the set M on the basis of which the relevance of the second conjunct is established. In the latter case, differences in the order of conjuncts will be accompanied by differences in interpretation: when the constituent conjuncts refer to events, a temporal or causal link between them could thus be implicated. More generally, the order in which propositions are expressed — whether co-ordinate or not — will affect the set of initial assumptions M on the basis of which the relevance of succeeding utterances is established. Hence something rather more explicit than the maxim of orderliness follows automatically from the principle of relevance.

To sum up the arguments of this section: two of the manner maxims ('Avoid ambiguity' and 'Be brief') seem to us to be eliminable, at least in their present form. We have argued that all the other maxims reduce to a principle of relevance which, by itself, makes clearer and more accurate predictions than the combined set of maxims succeeds in doing.

Finally, we have suggested that there is a corollary to the principle of relevance, which can be used to account for certain effects of linguistic form on the pragmatic interpretation of utterances — effects which Grice largely ignored.


## 4. Concluding Remark

Grice claims that a speaker who observes the conversational maxims will in general also be observing the Co-operative Principle (42):

(42) Make your conversational contribution such as is required, at the stage at which it occurs, by the accepted purpose or direction of the·talk-exchange in which you are engaged.

Would a theory in which Grice's maxims have, as we propose, been replaced by a principle of relevance and its corollary, also vindicate the Co-operative Principle?

It seems that the answer is no. Unlike the maxims, the principle of relevance does not follow from the Co-operative Principle. Obviously, it does not contradict it either: a theory which claimed that conversation was not a co-operative venture at all would be rather lacking in plausibility. However, it is not at all clear that it is *because* conversation is a co-operative venture that utterances are interpreted in the way they are. The account we are proposing might suggest rather that the speaker tries to have the maximum possible effect on the hearer's set of initial assumptions: a certain amount of co-operation is the price the speaker has to pay in order to succeed in this essentially egotistic enterprise. We do not want to defend this alternative view here: for one thing, it is extremely imprecise. However, we do want to draw attention to an important issue it raises: contrary to what Grice's theory leads one to expect, no clear moral or sociological principle emerges from the regularities that govern conversational behaviour.


## Notes

*A shorter version of this paper appeared in French in *Communications, 30* (1979) 80–94. We are grateful to Diane Brockway, Ruth Kempson, Geoff Pullum and Neil Smith for a number of helpful comments.
1. The term 'theory of conversation', though now standard, is really a misnomer. Grice's theory is in fact an account of how utterances are interpreted, and

not a theory of conversation at all: in the first place, it hardly touches on the characteristic alternation of roles in conversation, and in the second place, utterances which do not strictly form part of a conversation – for example lectures, articles, books – do fall within the scope of the maxims. See Grice (1968), (1975), (1978).

2. The maxims are stated in (32), (33), (35) and (36) below, and the Co-operative Principle in (42).

3. See, for example, Gazdar (1979), Kempson (1975), Wilson (1975), Harnish (1977), Morgan (1978) and Sadock (1978). In France, Ducrot (1972) has independently proposed a somewhat similar approach to Grice's.

4. Walker (1975) makes a similar point about disambiguation. The point is often overlooked: cf. Kaplan (1978), Stalnaker (1972), who suggest that context alone can determine disambiguation. This can clearly only be so to the extent that there is a highly constrained procedure for selecting a unique disambiguation, GIVEN a context. This procedure is what the maxims, and the assumption that they are being observed, seem to us to provide.

5. This new distinction has implications for the analysis of negative 'pre-supposition-carrying' utterances such as (i):

(i)  Lydia's sister didn't play a piano sonata.

(i) is standardly interpreted as presupposing (ii); the problem is to decide whether it is related to (ii) by semantic or pragmatic rule:

(ii) Lydia has a sister.

Within Grice's framework, there are only two possibilities: either (ii) is part of the conventional meaning of (i), related to it by semantic rule, or it is a conversational implicature of (i), related to it via the maxims of conversation. Both possibilities have been investigated in some detail (see Oh and Dinneen, eds., 1979, for a representative collection of papers). However, as suggested above, there is a third possibility: that (ii) is related to (i) as (5) is related to (4), neither by conventional meaning alone, nor as a conversational implicature: as part of the proposition the speaker of (i) is taken to have expressed, but not in virtue of the semantic rules alone.

Suppose that (i) is semantically interpreted as expressing the external negation (iii):

(iii)  It is not the case that Lydia has a sister who played a piano sonata.

Just as (6) is entailed by the more specific (5), so (iii) is entailed by the more specific internal negation (iv):

(iv)  Lydia has a sister who didn't play a piano sonata.

A properly defined maxim of informativeness could lead the hearer to interpret (i) as expressing (iv) rather than the less specific (iii), in just the same way as it leads him to interpret (4) as expressing (5) rather than the less specific (6). (ii) is neither entailed nor conversationally (nor conventionally) implicated by (i): it is part of the proposition the speaker is taken to have expressed, but a part not determined by semantic rules alone.

6. See Harnish (1977) for further discussion of this point.

7. Grice (1978) makes this point about irony, but his discussion of it is rather inconclusive.

8. See Sperber (1975), Sperber and Wilson (forthcoming a, forthcoming c), for an account of figurative language along the lines laid down in this section.

9. The logic used in deriving pragmatic implications must in fact be more restricted than standard logics in at least one respect: it must lack certain 'trivial' inference rules contained in most standard logics. The 'trivial' rules are those that (a) apply to any proposition at all, regardless of its form or content, and hence (b) may reapply an indefinite number of times given a single initial premise or pair of premises. With the exclusion of these rules, the pragmatic implications of a given proposition will always be finite, given a finite set of premises. For further discussion, see Sperber and Wilson (forthcoming b).

10. For a more detailed definition of relevance along these lines, together with discussion of some problems it might seem to raise, see Sperber and Wilson (forthcoming b).

11. A detailed account of the mechanisms involved is given in Wilson and Sperber (1979). We have no space to do more than mention them here.

# References

Bever, T., J.J. Katz and D.T. Langendoen (eds.) (1977) *An Integrated Theory of Linguistic Abilities*, Harvester Press, Brighton

Blackburn, S. (ed.) (1975) *Meaning, Reference and Necessity*, Cambridge University Press, Cambridge

Cole, P. (ed.) (1978) *Syntax and Semantics, 9: Pragmatics*, Academic Press, New York

—— and J. Morgan (eds.) (1975) *Syntax and Semantics, 3: Speech Acts*, Academic Press, New York

Davidson, D. and G. Harman (eds.) (1972) *Semantics of Natural Language*, Reidel, Dordrecht

Ducrot, O. (1972) *Dire et ne pas dire*, Hermann, Paris

Gazdar, G. (1979) *Pragmatics: Implicature, Presupposition and Logical Form*, Academic Press, New York

Grice, H.P. (1968) *William James Lectures*, unpublished mimeo

—— (1975) 'Logic and Conversation', in Cole and Morgan (1975)

—— (1978) 'Further Notes on Logic and Conversation', in Cole (1978)

Harnish, R.M. (1977) 'Logical Form and Implicature', in Bever, Katz and Langendoen (1977)

Kaplan, D. (1978) 'DTHAT', in Cole (1978)

Kempson, Ruth (1975) *Presupposition and the Delimitation of Semantics*, Cambridge University Press, Cambridge

Morgan, J.L. (1978) 'Two types of Convention in Indirect Speech Acts', in Cole (1978)

Oh, C-K. and D.A. Dinneen (eds.) (1979) *Syntax and Semantics, 11: Presupposition*, Academic Press, New York

Sadock, Jerrold (1978) 'On Testing for Conversational Implicature', in Cole (1978)

Sperber, Dan (1975) 'Rudiments de rhetorique cognitive', *Poétique, 23*, 389–415

—— and Deirdre Wilson (forthcoming a) 'Irony and the Use-Mention Distinction', to appear in P. Cole (ed.) *Radical Pragmatics*. Published in French in *Poétique, 36*, 399–412

—— and Deirdre Wilson (forthcoming b) *Foundations of Pragmatic Theory*

—— and Deirdre Wilson (forthcoming c) *Foundations of Rhetorical Theory*

Stalnaker, R. (1972) 'Pragmatics', in Davidson and Harman (1972)

Walker, Ralph (1975) 'Conversational Implicatures', in Blackburn (1975)

Wilson, Deirdre (1975) *Presuppositions and Non-Truth-Conditional Semantics*, Academic Press, London
—— and Dan Sperber (1979) 'Ordered Entailments: An Alternative to Presuppositional Theories', in Oh and Dinneen (1979)

# NOTES ON CONTRIBUTORS

Michael Brenner, Department of Social Studies, Oxford Polytechnic, England.

Chet A. Creider, Department of Anthropology, University of Western Ontario, Canada.

Hazel C. Emslie, Department of Psychology, University of Durham, England.

Allen D. Grimshaw, Department of Sociology, Indiana University, Bloomington, Indiana, USA.

Margaret MacLure, School of Education Research Unit, University of Bristol, England.

Martin Montgomery, School of Education Research Unit, University of Bristol, England.

Marion Owen, Department of Linguistics, University of Cambridge, England.

Dan Sperber, CNRS and Université de Paris X, Nanterre and Paris, France.

Rosemary J. Stevenson, Department of Psychology, University of Durham, England.

Gordon Wells, School of Education Research Unit, University of Bristol, England.

Paul Werth, Department of Linguistics, University of Hull, North Humberside, England, and (from October 1980) Institut de Phonétique, Université Libre de Bruxelles, Belgium.

Deirdre Wilson, Department of Phonetics and Linguistics, University College London, England.

# INDEX